Current Perspectives in Psychology

Family
Routines
and
Rituals

Barbara H. Fiese

YALE UNIVERSITY PRESS   NEW HAVEN AND LONDON

Set in Adobe Garamond by IBT Global.
Printed in the United States of America by IBT Global.

Library of Congress Cataloging-in-Publication Data

Fiese, Barbara H.
    Family routines and rituals / Barbara H. Fiese.
        p. cm. — (Current perspectives in psychology)
    Includes bibliographical references (p.   ) and index.
    ISBN-13: 978-0-300-11696-0 (alk. paper)

A catalogue record for this book is available from the British Library.
The paper in this book meets the guidelines for permanence and durability of the
Committee on Production Guidelines for Book Longevity of the Council on Library
Resources.

10 9 8 7 6 5 4

*To all the families who have made this work possible
and to my own for their support along the way*

Contents

Series Foreword

Current Perspectives in Psychology presents the latest discoveries and developments across the spectrum of the psychological and behavioral sciences. The series explores such important topics as learning, intelligence, trauma, stress, brain development and behavior, anxiety, interpersonal relationships, education, child-rearing, divorce and marital discord, and child, adolescent, and adult development. Each book focuses on critical advances in research, theory, methods, and applications and is designed to be accessible and informative to nonspecialists and specialists alike.

In this book, Barbara H. Fiese discusses the roles that routines, rituals, and activities play in family life. The strength of the book lies in the scope of routines and rituals that are covered and the breadth of their relations to mental and physical health of children, adolescents, and adults. Fiese covers how family routines have evolved in response to changes in family life and the roles they now occupy. Many different routines are discussed, including meals, conversation, celebrations, and holidays. Cultural and religious rituals are also discussed, as well as disruptions of routines in critical life transitions (marriage, divorce). Finally, the role of rituals in interventions, primarily psychotherapy, is highlighted to convey the broad role that rituals can play. The book is excellent in its coverage of research and well seasoned with case examples, vignettes, and dialogue between family members to illustrate key points. Dr. Barbara Fiese is without peer in her experience, research, and command of the topic. We are extremely fortunate to have such an authoritative statement on a topic with such breadth and relevance to children, families, and society at large.

Alan E. Kazdin
Series Editor

Preface

It seems somehow fitting that I write the Preface to this book over Thanksgiving weekend. The American tradition of Thanksgiving happens to be one of my favorite family holidays. The tradition revolves around food, telling family stories, and just relaxing as a group watching a football game or two after being well fed. The house is full of wonderful smells and anticipation for family gatherings. My family's heritage is evident in the platters pulled out once a year to serve the turkey, and the meal itself is a blending of old family recipes passed down across generations to ones that our family has created as our own. The conversation weaves old tales told every Thanksgiving with news of members returning after adventures away from home. Encapsulated in this gathering are markers of my own family's identity and feelings of being connected across generations.

I come from a family of storytellers, so it is with great pleasure that I have been able to spend much of my professional career hearing tales of family traditions from individuals participating in research conducted at the Family Research Lab housed at Syracuse University. Hundreds of families have invited us into their homes and shared with us the most intimate and challenging features of family life. To them, I owe special gratitude for making this work possible. The work conducted at the Family Research Lab has been supported by the National Institutes of Health, the John D. and Catherine T. MacArthur Foundation, the William T. Grant Foundation, the Spencer Foundation, and the March of Dimes Birth Defects Foundation. To these agencies, I acknowledge their support and trust in our laboratory to conduct this important research. I have been fortunate to work with highly talented undergraduate and graduate students over the past fifteen years and more recently with full-time staff at the Family Research Lab. The dedication, sensitivity, and good humor of all members of the lab have made this work not only possible but also a source of great satisfaction. In some ways it was risky to embark on a career of family research, particularly in an area that had received scant empirical attention. Without the support of senior researchers I could not have persevered. In particular, I acknowledge the steadfast support and wisdom of Arnold Sameroff, a highly valued mentor and friend. I have also been supported in innumerable ways by David Reiss and members of the Family Research Center at George Washington University. Ross Parke has provided valuable guidance and was pivotal in bringing the study of family rituals to the attention of family researchers through his editorship of the *Journal of Family Psychology*. The Family Narrative Consortium has evolved from a salon of scholars to some of my closest colleagues, and I continue to learn from Susan Dickstein, Hal Grotevant, and Fred Wamboldt. I am also thankful for Alan Kazdin's invitation to prepare this book. His encouragement has been a strong motivator throughout this project.

Through the many hours of burying myself in my study, my family has been patient and understanding. My parents, brother, husband, and son not only have taught me the value of family rituals but have done so in a way that always lets me know I am a member of a special group.

1

Routines of Daily Living and Rituals in Family Life

HUSBAND: Our weekends are pretty busy. By the time I arrive downstairs in the morning she's already cleaning up, vacuuming the floors, doing the laundry, and the coffee's already been made. I referee basketball, and it's all over the place, and my daughter plays soccer, so everybody has to work around different schedules. We try to do family events as well.

WIFE: It's not quite as organized, but we do plan meals and try to eat together on the weekend. A lot of times we go to my brother's for dinner on Sunday.

HUSBAND: The girls often help make the cheesecake.

WIFE: It's changed, though. The kids have gotten older; they have more involvements where they work more often. But now we really don't have as much control as we used to.

HUSBAND: But I think the kids still have very much enjoyment looking ahead to family events.

WIFE: We try to make those family events special to them.

HUSBAND: Yeah, it is different from in my family growing up. I tried to get away from them because there wasn't any family unity. I think I've been more encouraged to go in the direction of my wife's family. I look forward to that part.

WIFE: I always admired my parents for their having dinner at the table every night, working together to do that, making sure we were all there for dinner. So I've tried to do that. I think I've successfully accomplished that until up to the last couple of years. One's off to college and one's working, and so I think we did that pretty well. We just try to show them that they have to work for what they have, so I've tried to instill that you all have to work together, because my family did that. And then traditions, too, like Christmas and holidays and birthdays, those were always big in my family. It's a special time for the family. We make time to do that.

(Parents of children ranging in age from elementary school to college discussing family routines)

Most would agree that family life is complicated. But what makes it so? Perhaps it is the need to balance the needs of multiple individuals and their unique personalities. Or perhaps it is adjusting to the ever-shifting developmental changes that are part of the family life cycle. Or perhaps it is adapting to blending the heritage or cultures of two families through marriage. One of the ways in which families go about balancing, adjusting, and adapting to these multifaceted demands is through the organized practice of routines and the creation of meaningful rituals. This is a book about how variations in family routines and rituals support child development, are woven into the family life cycle, are related to physical and mental health, and are used in therapeutic interventions.

Family routines and rituals have been topics of interest to scholars from a variety of fields for some time. There are a multitude of reasons why there is such diversity in approaching this subject matter. As family members, we may want some helpful hints as to how to create rituals that can be sustained across time or how to find ways to infuse some fresh ideas into old traditions. In general, this book is not meant to serve as a catalogue of specific routines and rituals that families can incorporate into their daily lives. Although the examples provided in this book may spark ideas for some, each family defines what is important to them; that in turn gives meaning to their daily practices and special celebrations. The reader is referred to other source materials that describe particular family traditions (Cox 2003; Lieberman 1991; Walter 1995).

Historians and sociologists have found the study of rituals useful in understanding how changes in the workforce and economic conditions influence local and community-wide celebrations. Often these studies are aimed at examining "high-profile public" rituals such as community-wide festivals and public observances of religious holidays. They also focus on how shifts in economic conditions alter the practices of home-based rituals (see Pleck 2000, for discussion of this last point). Although we certainly consider how changing economic conditions, such as maternal work roles, affect family routines, we are primarily interested in the more intimate routines and rituals of family life that may be hidden from public view. In this regard, our journey explores the more sublime and mundane aspects of family life that hold special meaning for its members.

Anthropologists have also turned their attention to the role that rituals play in families. Margaret Mead's seminal observations of the customs and rites in Samoa were influential in our understanding of adolescent development in the family context (Mead 1928). Anthropological literature tends to focus on specific rites and customs and how they reflect broader organization of the culture. Although we will consider how culture influences family rituals, we do so in the context of its influence on individual health and well-being and family relationships rather than as a catalogue of cultural values per se.

Theoretical Framework

Portions of this book focus on how family routines and rituals are reflective of larger processes such as the family life cycle, developmental regulation, and behavior change. Each of these topics is worthy of attention in its own right and has been the subject of many fine texts. It is important to emphasize that family routines and rituals are not necessarily the *only* or even the most parsimonious way to understand family effects on individual growth and development. Certainly such features as parental warmth, responsiveness, and consistent patterns of discipline offer strong avenues of influence. The study of family routines and rituals can be considered a midlevel approach to studying family organization (Howe 2002). Rather than focusing on global indices of family order, the study of family routines and rituals points to patterns of organization and interaction that may be important for individual development. In this book I propose that family routines and rituals make sense to families, they afford the possibility of examining both how families *act* and what they *believe,* they mark important transitions in family life, and they may be used systematically in therapeutic interventions. In this regard, I aim to examine how the practice of family routines and meaning ascribed to family rituals provides access to how this important group is organized and how group and individual processes transact with each other.

A nagging problem in family studies is how to capture group process as a whole. Much of what we know about family effects on development arises from observations and reports of dyadic relationships. In developmental psychology, there is a long history documenting the importance of mother-child interaction patterns and the attachment relationship (Bowlby, 1967). More recently, fathers have been included in these studies (Parke and O'Neil 1999). Family researchers are also interested in the effects of the marital dyad on child development. For example, how husbands and wives resolve conflict may influence how children regulate their own affect and, under some conditions, may place them at risk for developing behavioral problems (Cummings, Davies, and Campbell 2000). Although the study of dyadic relationships is important to the field of family research, it does not capture the essence of family life. Families are organic wholes whose compositions shift with birth, death, marriage, divorce, and remarriage. As a stabilizing force, families create rules for behavior and make it clear what is acceptable to be a member of the group. As a holding place, families provide comfort, nurturance, and a secure base from which to develop individual autonomy. A resolvable tension in the study of families is how to integrate the strivings and perceptions of the individual into the communal boundaries of the group. This tension is resolvable in that the study of family routines and rituals allows us to examine not only how the individual perceives his or her place in the family but also how the family, as a group, regulates behavior in response to the individual. This is very much a transactional process whereby characteristics of individual members contribute to the functioning of the group (Sameroff and Fiese 2000).

Let us consider three points that will guide much of the discussion throughout this book: (1) families change; (2) change occurs as part of a transactional process; and (3) both family practices and beliefs contribute to the health and well-being of individual members.

By their very nature, families are defined by change through shifts in membership (marriage, birth, death). What is central to the framework of this book is that some change is expectable and geared toward regulating optimal development. Much of the work I cite draws upon developmental research, mostly that of child development. From this vantage point, a key concern might be how the family organizes the child's daily routines so that he or she establishes regular sleep patterns, feeding routines, and bedtime routines in the first three years of life. From the perspective of developmental psychology, it is important to understand not only how these activities evolve but also how they are related to such important outcomes as transition to school, behavior regulation, and mental health. In this regard, we examine the rhythms of daily life for their stability, their alterations during developmental transitions, and how they predict later adjustments.

Some types of family change are not anticipated, however, and also bring challenges to daily organization. The death of a family member, diagnosis of a chronic illness, or even relocation to a new geographic location affect all family members and call for a reassignment of roles and reconsideration of rituals. In some instances, families can use rituals as a mechanism to reduce the stresses associated with unanticipated change. In other instances, the added stresses disrupt rituals to the extent that they come close to extinction or hollow in practice.

Change must also be understood in context. A widely accepted model of developmental change is the transactional model originally proposed by Sameroff and Chandler (Sameroff and Chandler 1975). At the core of this model is the notion that developmental adaptation and functioning at any given time is the result of a series of transactions between child and parent over time. Not only does the parent affect the child, but the child's behavior also affects the parent. For example, a child born prematurely may be at risk for developing delays in language development. If the caregiver is responsive to the child's signals and the child engages in vocal play, however, a series of transactions is set in place such that language develops at an age appropriate pace (Sameroff and Fiese 2000). The child's contribution to the exchange is equally important as the caregiver's responsiveness. For our purposes, we note that individuals influence family organization through their developmental features and personalities and that the family, as an organized group, influences the development of the individual. I will present several examples where a given outcome, such as school performance or the health of an individual, is the result of a series of transactions between the organization of family routines or the affective investment in family rituals and characteristics of the individual.

This transactional regulation is also embedded within a cultural context. The goals of development and types of behavior supported within the family context may vary systematically across cultures. For example, there are different timetables for weaning infants from breastfeeding. Feeding routines may be altered by cultural norms of when weaning is expected to occur (Dettwyler 1987). The parent may thus read the child's hunger signals and begin to introduce a bottle or finger food at different points in time, which in turn will create new feeding routines and provide opportunities for different types of social interaction.

The third point to consider is that both family practices and beliefs are important in examining the interaction between family process and individual adjustment. This may seem intuitively obvious; however, these domains draw upon two traditions in family research and family therapy. Sometimes referred to as the practicing or representing family (Reiss 1989), family practices are considered directly observable behaviors, and family representations are considered internally held meanings or beliefs that in turn affect behavior. From the standpoint of the practicing family, identifiable patterns of social interactions are proposed to influence behavior.

Notable among programs of research in this tradition has been the work of G. R. Patterson and colleagues, who have identified coercive patterns of parenting practices related to antisocial behavior problems in youth (G. R. Patterson 1982). Through a series of home- and laboratory-based observations, these researchers and clinicians have been able to identify a pattern of family interactions that predict antisocial behavior from the early school years into adulthood. The pattern evolves from the parent and child engaging in what is initially an expectable situation where the child is asked to comply with a parent's request. The interaction deteriorates to the point where the child is clearly in control. For example, a parent may ask the child to turn off the television and go to bed. The child refuses and pleads for an additional ten minutes. The parent gives in. Ten minutes later the child whines, and the parent gives the child an additional ten minutes. Ten more minutes pass, the child throws a temper tantrum, and the parent gives the child another ten minutes. When the child is still not in bed thirty minutes later, the parent has reached his or her limit and may give in or punish the child. (Four out of five times the parent gives in.) The child learns this coercive pattern of interacting to get what he or she wants and then applies the same tactics to peers and in school settings. This line of research led clinicians to develop inter- ventions aimed at changing parenting behaviors with the expectation that child behavior problems would be ameliorated (Martinez and Forgatch 2001; G. R. Patterson, DeGarmo, and Forgatch 2004).

The point is that what we learn about family process from this vantage point is based solely on what we directly observe. These in- teraction patterns are typically repeated over time and tend to be rela- tively stable. In the case of family routines we can directly observe how families conduct their daily activities and consider changes in activi- ties across time. In this regard, we tap into family practices through the study of family routines.

A second tradition in family studies is a focus on family beliefs, or representations of relationships. From this standpoint, the inter- pretations or beliefs held about a set of behaviors are proposed to guide development and regulate family process. A notable example of this perspective is in the tradition of attachment theory and work- ing models of relationships (Bowlby 1967). Again, briefly and simply put, relationships between the infant and the caregiver are formed early in development. Patterns of relationships are identified based on observations of interactions between infant and caregiver and in detailed interviews about close relationships. Relationships that are considered secure develop from responsive parenting and protection from harm. Belief systems are created such that relationships are seen as trustworthy and there is an expectation that others can be relied upon. Insecure relationships, by contrast, develop from inconsistent and at times harsh and controlling parenting. Under these conditions, belief systems are created such that others are seen as potential sources of harm and disappointment. These beliefs then guide behavior and have been linked to the establishment of peer relationships (Carlson, Sroufe, and Egeland 2004) and the type of marital relationships formed (Dickstein, Seifer, St. Andre, and Schiller, 2001), and they often extend across generations (Fiese and Marjinsky, 1999).These observations then lead clinicians to focus on altering beliefs or internally held meanings about relationships to relieve emotional distress (Fonagy 2000).

Family therapists have had a long-standing interest in the meanings behind what family members communicate to each other. Many speculate that these "hidden meanings" are reflections of the unspoken beliefs that guide behavior. Families express their own senses of reality through communications that are thick with symbolic referents. Therapists often attend to the symbolic significance of how family members use language and address each other. When a fifty-year-old woman is referred to as "Little Sis," the therapist wants to know how this moniker reflects her standing in the family and whether it may be related to her continued dependence on her aging parents. Other forms of symbolism in the family communicate deeply held meanings, such as nicknames, family stories, or family jokes. In recognizing that family beliefs may also affect individual development and well-being, we must also consider the insider's view of family life. In this regard, family rituals or the affective investment and symbolic meaning behind these gatherings reflect family beliefs that may affect behavior.

Traditionally, family process has been studied with a lens toward either directly observed behaviors or internally held beliefs. Each approach has its own rich traditions embedded in behaviorism on one hand, and psychodynamic theory on the other. It is well beyond the scope of this book, and indeed beyond the reach of the science of family routines and rituals, to offer a single unifying theory that addresses the subtle and complex ways in which behavior and beliefs operate simultaneously in families. What we can consider, however, is under what conditions family routines may be most closely related to which aspects of health and well-being and under what conditions the symbolic meaning of family rituals is most closely connected to individual outcomes. We can also examine whether an alteration in routines may lead to more optimal adjustment or whether ritual interventions are warranted. As we consider different types of interventions in Chapter 7 we note that it is unlikely that a "one size fits all" answer will be satisfactory.

In sum, this book has broad-reaching goals. First, it aims to integrate the empirical literature on family routines and rituals that resides primarily in developmental psychology, interpersonal relations, family systems, and family therapy. Second, it strives to provide a framework for the reader to evaluate the potential for family routines and rituals to be used systematically in promoting mental and physical health in terms of both prevention and therapeutic interventions. Third, it calls upon the reader to consider whether the "whole of the family" as represented in its routines and rituals is greater than any of its individual parts.

Throughout the book I have incorporated examples drawn from interviews conducted with families in several studies conducted at the Family Research Lab at Syracuse University. We have been fortunate that so many families have agreed to allow us into their homes or have come to our laboratory to share their experiences. I present examples from these very personal interviews. I have changed names, places, and other identifying pieces of information to protect these valued participants. The intent of the messages, however, remains the same.

Defining Family Routines and Rituals

Most researchers active in the study of family routines and rituals agree that operationally defining routines and rituals is a challenge at best (Boyce, Jensen, James, and Peacock 1983; van der Hart 1983; Wolin and Bennett 1984). This challenge has many sources. First, all families and family members likely have their own definitions of what

constitutes a routine or a ritual. Indeed, this personalized and individualized aspect of family organization may provide special meaning to
group activities and gatherings. Second, rituals are highly symbolic in
nature. They are dense with physical, patterned, and affective symbols.
Rituals have been described as the "deep structure" of family relationships that "affirm the reality of abstract meanings for daily living, and
they define the continuity of experience between past, present, and
future" (Cheal 1988b, 638).

Routines and rituals can be contrasted along the dimensions of
communication, commitment, and continuity (table 1.1). Routines
typically involve instrumental communication conveying what needs
to be done. The language of routines is direct, implies action, and
often includes designation of roles. Routines involve momentary
time commitment and are more often associated with episodic rather
than semantic memory. Once the act is completed there is little after-
thought, and there is an uninterrupted flow to daily life. Routines are
repeated over time, with little alteration, and can be directly observed
by outsiders.

Rituals, by contrast, involve symbolic communication and signify this is "who we are as a group." The language of rituals is multilayered such that what may appear to the outsider as a mundane phrase
may be dense with meaning for family members. There is an affective
commitment to rituals that provides feelings of belonging and knowing that you fit in. Often, the elements of a ritual will be played over
in memory before and after the event. Rituals have a liminal phase
that places the event as "a moment in and out of time" (Turner, 1969,
96). These symbolic gatherings are organized around multiple elements: the preparatory phase, the event, and reminiscence. Different
elements may overlap such that the preparatory phase may include
reminiscence of previous occasions, leaving the individual with a sense
of bridging two timeframes—those between past and future generations. Thus, there is a generational continuity to rituals such that they
encapsulate family identity and investment in how the family will
continue to be.

When routines are disrupted, it is a hassle. Someone forgets to
stop at the grocery store after work, so there is no milk for breakfast
cereal. When rituals are disrupted, the group's cohesion is threatened.

Table 1.1. Definitions of Routines and Rituals

Characteristic	Routines of daily living	Rituals in family life
Communication	Instrumental: "This is what needs to be done."	Symbolic: "This is who we are."
Commitment	Perfunctory and momentary: little conscious thought given after the act.	Enduring and affective: "This is right." The experience may be repeated in memory.
Continuity	Directly observable and detectable by outsiders. Behavior is repeated over time.	Meaning extends across generations and is interpreted by insiders: "This is what we look forward to and who we will continue to be across generations."

Source: Reprinted from Fiese et al. (2002), A review of 50 years of research in naturally occurring family routines and rituals: Cause for celebration? *Journal of Family Psychology, 16,* 381–390.

At the beginning of the movie *Avalon* (1990, directed by Barry Levinson), the family is seen gathered around the dining table for a Thanksgiving feast. As is the tradition in many American families, the focus of the celebration is on the meal itself, where the menu rarely changes (turkey, stuffing, potatoes, green beans, pumpkin pie). The tradition in this family also includes waiting for all the adult brothers and sisters to arrive with their children before the celebration can start. Everyone is hungry but waits for the last brother (routinely late) to arrive. Only then is the family fully assembled, and the meal can continue. A year later, the family is seen again at the Thanksgiving table waiting for the ever-late brother. This time, however, the family begins to eat before the brother arrives. Once the brother arrives he notes that the family is already eating and storms out of the house, remarking, "You cut the turkey without me! I can't believe you cut the turkey without me." He leaves the home, never to return. Granted, a multitude of events led up to this point. The disruption of the ritual was but one marker of the threats to the family as a whole.

Rituals and routines don't happen only in the movies. To illustrate the distinction between the two, let us examine mealtimes and the simultaneous expression of directly observable practices and indirectly inferred symbolic meaning.

Mealtime Routines

A headline of the *Christian Scientist Monitor* read, "Reports of De-mise of Family Dinner Hour Are Greatly Exaggerated" (Wolcott 2001). Families with children under age eighteen eat dinner together always or frequently 77 percent of the time. This report is consistent with epidemiological surveys where family members report that they eat together at least three to four times a week (Eisenberg, Olson, Neumark-Sztainer, Story, and Bearinger 2004). Typically, these are not elaborate affairs but last, on average, twenty minutes (Ramey and Juliusson 1998). Several routine elements are evident in family meal-times (table 1.2).

Seat Assignment

First is seat assignment. For a meal to begin, everyone needs to know where to sit. A recurring theme in several of our interviews is parents' descriptions of seat assignments at mealtime and how to rearrange family members if there is a disruption.

> We all have our own seats—unless we have company, and then there is a big discussion about who gets to sit next to the guest, and the guest gets to sit in the middle if there is one guest. Otherwise, we'll have them make name cards. They love to do that, so that everyone has a seat.
>
> Confusion rules when my husband is not home be-cause it's "who's gonna sit where?" Because it's this big empty spot down there, and the children don't like that. Of course, none of us like that. So who fills in where, and who sits where, and then mommy is in the middle this time, and everybody shifts and shuffles around. I might say, "I'll be daddy today." But it is amazing it makes such a huge difference.

Manners

Mealtime routines often include expectations for manners and ac-ceptable conduct. In a small study of eight families with preschool

Table 1.2. Routine and Ritual Aspects of Mealtime

	Routine	Ritual
Seat Assignment	Who sits where?	Who is at the "head" of the table?
Manners	Say "please" and "thank you"	What is acceptable conduct in *our* family?
Role assignment	Who does what?	Gendered and developmental expectations
Conversational turn-taking	Use of "rare" words Vocabulary building	Provides opportunity to explore sensitive topics in safe and secure environment
Attendance	Who will be home for dinner?	Who is "in" and "out" of the family

children, fourteen and a half politeness routines, on average, were observed per family per mealtime (Gleason, Perlmann, and Greif 1984). Interestingly, many of these routines were parental directives meant to regulate the child's behavior, such as "Don't wipe your mouth on your sleeve" or "Say the magic word." These directly observable and repetitive routines may impart cultural mores of expected behavior (Goodnow 1997). They may also serve a linguistic purpose in broadening the child's vocabulary.

Mealtimes can also be opportunities for problem solving and resolving conflict. In a study of sixty-four family dinners with families ranging in size from two to six and the children in the families, on average, twelve years of age, parents and children were equally likely to initiate conflict, and most bouts of conflict were relatively short but frequent (Vuchinich 1987). In most cases, conflict at the table ended in a standoff. Rather than considering this as an incomplete resolution, standoff resolution saved face and did not further disrupt the meal, as is the case when a family member withdraws from communicating altogether. Many of these conflicts are relatively mundane and thus do not imply a particularly hostile environment. One cited example was "Quit eating with your fingers" (Vuchinich 1987, 594). Even in the face of conflict, mealtime exchanges provide not only an opportunity to attend to good manners but also a context in which members feel that their voices will be heard.

Role Assignment

Family mealtimes are also noted for their division of labor (Dreyer and Dreyer 1973), with even contemporary surveys reporting that female members of the household are most likely to be responsible for preparing the meal. Routine housework chores of cooking, cleaning, and shopping are frequently described as "female-dominated" (Blair and Lichter 1991) or simply as "female" (Presser 1994). Even with a decrease in overall time that women spend on household chores during the week, women on average spend three times the amount of time on routine housework as the average man spends (Coltrane 2000). In many cases, women take on the role of home manager and are the architects of such daily family activities as mealtime.

Research involving direct observation of families at mealtime confirms routine role assignments mentioned in surveys and interviews. In a mealtime study of forty-six families (primarily middle- and upper-middle class) and their preschool-age children, the researchers found that mothers were most likely to serve the food, children were served first and ate first, and younger children were helped in eating (Fiering and Lewis 1987). The larger the family size, the more likely that there would be movement up and down from the table, and the less likely there would be a mutual ending to the meal.

In a larger study of 339 families with school-age children, mealtime similarities and differences were noted across families with married, divorced, and single parents (Ramey and Juliusson 1998). Across all family types, dinnertimes were marked by high rates of social engagement among all family members. In single-parent families, children were more likely to initiate engagement with their parent, and single parents engaged in more social interaction with their children than their married counterparts. This may be due in part to not having another adult to interact with, since married couples spend about 25 percent of the mealtime interacting with each other. When considering all the content of the exchanges among all family members, there were few differences across the groups. More than half of the time is spent in general positive exchanges, approximately 20 percent of the time is directed toward family management issues, and approximately 10 percent of the time is directed toward meal-related behavior. The authors conclude that even with the shifting demographics of family structure, mealtime behavior engages family members in a predictable and supportive way.

Conversational Turn-Taking

Mealtime conversations are noted as opportunities to reinforce vocabulary development and rules for conversational turn-taking. Children of parents who incorporate "rare" words at the dinner table such as "wriggling" score higher on standardized vocabulary tests (Beals and Snow 1994). Adolescents who regularly eat dinner with their family receive better grades than those who do not (Eisenberg et al. 2004). Thus, something as simple as saying "please" and "thank you" or a discussion about how asparagus grows ultimately may be associated with better academic performance. Certainly other factors need to be considered. The point here is that the seemingly mundane and apparently unconscious aspects of family routines are rooted in cultural expectations for child growth and development.

Dinnertime can also be considered a "familial speech event" whereby the collective gathering is associated with such socialization goals as good manners conveyed through social discourse (Blum-Kulka 1997). At its most basic level, conducting the meal involves verbal directives ("Pass the salt and pepper"; "May I have some more?"). Children are also encouraged to tell their news of the day and participate in family-level discussions about what happened in the neighborhood or to the family cat. When guests are present, there is also the opportunity for sharing family fables and tales of experience that define family relationships and connections across generations.

Attendance

A fifth routine characteristic of mealtimes is expectations for attendance. In our interviews with families we have noted that this aspect may have undergone changes over the past fifty years. Many parents recall that everyone was expected to be home at a certain time, but with shifting work schedules and after-school activities, expectations for attendance have become more flexible.

When I was growing up we would eat as soon as everyone got home from work, like between five and six. And on Saturdays, usually around seven or so, and then Sundays was always at one o'clock. Now we are a little more flexible. We usually try to eat between five and seven. And some nights my husband isn't home and one of the other kids is working. It might not be a big dinner, it may just be something I throw together, but usually I try to make dinner. And the kids try and help me set the table and do the dishes. It's a little bit tougher time-wise to plan what we are going to do at six o'clock because my husband may be arriving from out of town late. They need time to greet him. Our older daughter might have to work to 5:30 or 6:00, and the other kids have things after school. But usually I try to make a meal most every night. And on the weekends, usually Saturday night we try and do something, like all get together for dinner. We have a dinner on Saturday and then a big meal on Sunday. Sometimes it is one or the other, sometimes both.

In this brief example, there is a commitment to having dinner together but also the recognition that not everyone will be home and timing of the meal will be variable. It is interesting to note that the Saturday and Sunday meals play a role much like they did in this woman's family of origin.

Mealtime Rituals

The routines just described may also have symbolic and ritual components. Where family members sit at the table may reflect a hierarchical organization in the family. Parents sit at either end of the table, signifying their relative power over children sitting in the middle. During special meal gatherings, seat assignment may also reflect who is considered an elder and who is considered a child in the family. No doubt, readers can recall when they moved from the child's table to sit with the adults during a holiday gathering. Designation of "child" and "adult" in these gatherings is based not as much on chronological age as on whether the individual can be trusted to hear the stories of the older generation and be prepared to carry on traditions with future generations.

Manners may also hold symbolic content. Cultural mores include beliefs about acceptable and unacceptable behavior at the dinner table. In a study of families with infants and toddlers of four different American cultural groups, differences were observed in expectations for acceptable behavior during a mealtime (Martini 2002). The four groups all lived in Hawaii and self-identified either as Japanese-American, Caucasian-American, Hawaiian-American, or Filipino-American. Filipino-Americans were the most structured in their approach to the meal and held high expectations for obedience and respect for authority. Caucasian-American mothers were the least strict and viewed their infants' disruptive mealtime behaviors as signs of intelligence or strong will. Hawaiian-American parents were the most tolerant of allowing their infants and toddlers to roam during mealtime as long as it did not disrupt group interaction. Japanese-American parents were most likely to use redirection as a strategy if their child engaged in undesirable behaviors (for example, throwing food). Within-culture variability in expectations for manners is also noted in Western culture, where some families may have rules for quiet during the mealtime prayer, a set order as to who gets to talk first, or tolerance for belching or other such antics at the table.

Role assignment may signify gendered roles in the family, as previously noted. How roles are assigned may also signify when children reach different stages of responsibility. Setting and clearing the table, doing the dishes, and preparing meals are part of household chores. By the time children are, on average, between three and five years of age, they engage in some form of household work between five and six hours a week (Hofferth and Sandberg 2001). Women continue to be primarily responsible for carrying out the majority of household chores, regardless of whether they work outside the home (Coltrane 2000). When women are employed in demanding work they are more likely to call upon their daughters than their sons in assisting with routine work at home (Crouter, Head, Bumpus, and McHale 2001). Women also ascribe more meaning to such routine tasks as meal preparation and feel that preparing family meals is an important and valued activity (Kroska 2003). Thus, gendered roles supported in the culture are also supported in the enactment of mealtime roles.

The meaning behind repetitive topics at the table may reflect aspects of family identity and opportunities to reinforce family values. Mealtime conversations are opportunities to discuss sensitive topics and assure others that the family setting is a safe place. The following example is drawn from a previously published mealtime conversation between a mother and son where the topic was monsters and nightmares. The mother used the opportunity to direct the topic of the conversation to imagination and safety.

> MOTHER: You know I would never let any monsters get you. Besides, what did I tell you about monsters?
> SON: What?
> MOTHER: They're only make-believe, and they only live in movies because someone with a wonderful imagination makes up monsters . . . because someone has a great imagination.
> SON: Hmm.
> MOTHER: But no, there is no such thing as monsters.
> [Beals and Snow 1994, 76–77]

Mealtime conversations are not only a social activity where talking is an end in itself, but also a time of socialization of family values (Blum-Kulka 1997). Mealtime conversations may include a cultural code embedded in the flow of conversation. Sometimes, what is *not* said is as revealing as what *is* said. It has been observed that when children are present, money, sex, and politics are never discussed (Blum-Kulka 1997). These conversations highlight not only acceptable behaviors as in expectations for good manners but also sociocultural norms.

Failure to show up for an important family meal may signify who is "in" and "out" of the family. Surely the reader can recall planned family events where the absence of a family member is noted. For example, this often occurs following the death of a family member, and their absence is sorely felt. In other instances, an individual may have deliberately chosen not to attend a gathering due to strongly held convictions either that he or she had been wronged by the family or that an individual in the family was making a bad choice—such as in a marriage or remarriage.

Some meals are set aside as a special time. In our interviews, weekend meals were often anticipated and noted for their out-of-the-ordinary nature. Often they included more deliberate planning, a conscious setting aside from the rest of the week, and expectations that everyone would be present. Over time, these gatherings come to have meaning and define the family as a group. Indirectly, the emotion and affect present at these meals may come to symbolize what it means to be a member of a particular family.

Lest the reader be concerned that these multilayered aspects of mealtime are restricted to elaborate gatherings or must occur over extended periods of time, the following transcript of a mealtime conversation illustrates points such as role assignment, problem solving, and emotional commitments. This meal lasted thirty-nine minutes, so it may not be representative of most mealtimes we have observed. This family consists of a father, mother, twelve-year-old daughter, and seven-year-old son.

> DAD: What'd you do at school today, Johnson?
> BROTHER: I got my desk rearranged. And Mrs. Craft didn't yell at me.
> DAD: Was that for a good reason or a bad reason?
> BROTHER: Good.
> DAD: A reward?
> BROTHER: The whole class was moved into new groups.
> SISTER: Dad, we had groups, but now we are in rows.
> MOM: They are all connected?
> SISTER: Yeah.
> MOM: Who do you sit near?
> SISTER: Franklin.
> MOM: Oh, no way.
> SISTER: Yeah.
> MOM: Do you sit near Michael?
> SISTER: Noooo.
> [Family laughs]

DAD: Michael who?
SISTER: The one with the brown hair.
DAD: Is he a nice boy?
SISTER: He's annoying.
MOM: Is there a boy you know that's not annoying?
SISTER: No.
BROTHER: Me.
DAD: Johnson, tell the truth.
BROTHER: I'm not annoying!
DAD: You are the king of annoying.
[Family laughs]

The meal begins with a catch-up on the day's events as well as identifying different roles that family members play. Throughout the meal there is conversation about who is annoying, who is weird, and what being weird signifies. The conversation continues.

DAD: That was an interesting aspect of dinner with the camera running.
MOM: Can you imagine if Uncle Jess was at this dinner?
BROTHER: Cool!
SISTER: Don't serve beans when there is a camera around.
DAD: I don't think we want a camera with Uncle Jess. He's a barbarian.
[Family laughs]
DAD: He doesn't use silverware.
SISTER: See, that's the whole point. Don't serve green beans because if he puts them up his nose and looks at the camera.
DAD: And then everyone would know our family secrets. One thing we want to make sure they know is that's Mommy's brother. That is not Daddy's relation. Let's clarify that for the camera.
MOM: We love Uncle Jess.

BROTHER: Yeah.

SISTER: He's your brother-in-lawwwww.

DAD: I wasn't born with him. I just sorta married into the family.

MOM: I picked him out from the brother store.

DAD: Jess's Jess. He's a good guy.

MOM: He is a good boy.

In this segment of the conversation, the family discusses a relative who is not present but is clearly considered slightly different than the rest. However, being different doesn't mean that the family doesn't care for him, just that he possesses unusual characteristics. It is also interesting to note that the father brings up the distinction between being "born with him" and marrying into the family. In this brief comment, he reinforces family membership and perhaps some underlying meanings associated with family identities connected through biological versus relational heritages. The mealtime conversation ends with reference to how parents and children share similar personality characteristics.

[Family is eating ice cream and daughter has put sprinkles on peanut butter ice cream, which father considers disgusting.]

SISTER: Mmm peach is yummy, Mommy, try it.

MOM: I did.

DAD: She did.

SISTER: Oh.

DAD: It is good . . . but not with sprinkles.

SISTER: Well, that's your opinion.

DAD: OK, Meredith, how's the peanut butter ice cream and sprinkles?

SISTER: Yummy.

DAD: It is not yummy. C'mon, tell me the truth.

SISTER: But it's a little better without.

DAD: Haha! Thank you.

SISTER: Just a little bit.

DAD: Sprinkles aren't so good on peanut butter are they?

BROTHER: Sprinkles give it more taste.

DAD: OK, just admit it, ice cream is much better without the sprinkles.

SISTER: I never said so!

MOM: Just a slight improvement better.

DAD: Just slight improvement. Like Mommy.

MOM: Why do you exaggerate, Dad?

BROTHER: So that's where I got that from.

DAD: Got what?

BROTHER: The exaggeration.

MOM: Did you know you exaggerate?

DAD: You got that all by yourself. You didn't get that from me.

BROTHER: So you got it from me.

MOM: Imagine that, honey.

DAD: Yeah, I probably learned from the best.

MOM: You probably did.

DAD: He's worse than I am.

SISTER: It's just like when you always say fifty thousand. Like there were fifty thousand people there.

MOM: You think?

DAD: I don't think so.

In this closing conversation, the mother and daughter align themselves in liking sprinkles on their ice cream but also in their shared view of the father as tending to exaggerate. The son tries to align with the father through affirming his tendency toward exaggeration as well.

There are apparent generational influences on these practices. In a study of fifty families with school-age children, we asked parents to tell their children a story about a dinnertime when they were growing up. We reasoned that dinnertime, as a ritual, is passed down through generations and that expectations for positive and rewarding relationships should signify feelings of belonging to a group where one is a valued member. We contrast two of these stories.

Story 1

I remember a dinnertime when it was Christmas or something like that, and Mamma would bring out a huge turkey, and we would have ham, and beets, and homemade biscuits. And we would sit around and eat. And there was my aunt, uncle, grandmother, grandfather, and cousins, too. I remember my uncle would say a prayer before dinner, bless our food and our family. Or my grandfather might say it. My grandfather was a deacon in the church, and I always loved it when my grandfather said the prayer: "Jesus wept." And that was it, and we just dove in, and that was it. Sometimes there would be other kids over, and we would have a little table in the corner where we would eat, the kids, while the adults had the big table to themselves. And I remember that being a specially nice time. A lot of laughing, and cutting, and scraping, and eating, and talking, and all those kinds of good things.

Story 2

I remember—I can remember playing outside and my mother calling us in for dinner and we'd be like, "Oh Man." Nobody ever wanted to go in when it was dinnertime. We'd go in, and it seemed like my mother made steak every day, and when we were little we were made to eat—usually if my father was sitting there, we had to eat what was on the plate. If we were made to eat, we'd have to sit there until it was bedtime and eat that food. And if we didn't eat the food, we went to bed.

In the first story, the holiday meal is eagerly anticipated and there is a feeling of belonging to the group. There are symbolic signs as well, with the world's shortest prayer being easily identified by members of the family. In contrast, the second story paints a picture of the family meal as something that is endured, and anticipation is linked to the ending rather than to an opportunity to be with others. We found not only that these stories reflected how parents felt about mealtimes in

their families of origin but also that these themes of positive or negative family relationships were related to how the family interacted at
the dinner table and reports of child behavior problems. Families that
depicted mealtimes as sources of rewarding relationships displayed
more positive affect during a routine mealtime and had children with
fewer behavior problems than families who depicted mealtimes as opportunities for conflict and disregard (Fiese and Marjinsky 1999).

Supportive and Disruptive
Elements of Routines and Rituals

The astute reader will have noted that routines and rituals can have
both supportive and disruptive effects. Throughout this book I will
examine how routines can be used to structure time, to develop management strategies, and as a source of support to others. There are instances, however, where routines are disrupted and there can be a cost
to the family as a whole as well as to the functioning of the individual.
Under disruptive conditions, routines are often expressed as hassles,
obligations, or opportunities for escalating conflict.

The symbolic meaning of rituals can also be supportive or disruptive. Supportive rituals hold meanings of belonging to the group and
emotional commitments. However, as has been noted, family rituals
can also be opportunities for exclusion and devaluing the opinions
and feelings of others. Under these conditions, the individual is more
likely to want to disengage rather than promote the continuation of a
particular family ritual (table 1.3).

Thus far, I have presented family routines and rituals as clearly
distinct from each other. This may not always be the case. As later
chapters will show, the repetition of routines over time sometimes creates the foundation for a ritual through eager anticipation and emotional investment. One way to know whether a routine has developed
into a family ritual is if its absence would be missed and noted by
family members. The flip side of this question is whether a ritual has
turned into a routine by its sense of dreaded obligation. When I examine the therapeutic use of rituals in Chapter 7, I note that tensions
can arise when a sense of obligation outweighs the potential emotional
connections that can be made during a family ritual. As families face

Table 1.3. Supportive and Disruptive Elements of Routines and Rituals

	Routine activities	Ritual meanings
Supportive	Management strategies	Belonging to the group
	Structure	Emotional containment
	Demarks time	Commitment to the future
	Supported by others	Emotional lineage
	Planning	Consecration of the past
Disruptive	Rigid or chaotic	Alienation
	Resentments and obligations	Degradation
	Pressed for time	Exclusion
	Depleted energy	Coercion
	Explosive or conflictual interactions	Cutting off emotional expression

normative developmental transitions or non-normative stresses such as coping with an illness or poverty, stress to the system is often revealed in how the family balances the organization of daily routines and emotional investment of rituals. In some cases, routines become a burden or a chore. In other cases, rituals become hollow and meaningless. I will return to this point after a further review of the literature.

Routine and Ritual Settings

I have used mealtime as an example of a family gathering that includes both routine and ritual components. Other settings also constitute regular family gatherings. There are three commonly accepted categories of family rituals: family celebrations, family traditions, and patterned family interactions (Wolin and Bennett 1984). Family celebrations are holidays and occasions widely practiced throughout a culture that hold special meaning for the family. These events may include such rites of passage as baptisms, weddings, and funerals. Religious celebrations associated with such holidays as Christmas, Easter, and Passover are also family celebrations.

Family traditions are less culture specific and tied more closely to the unique characteristics of a family. These gatherings may include vacations, birthday traditions, and anniversary celebrations. In our interviews of families with school-age children, we find that many of these traditions are passed down from one generation to the next. Parents recall holding on to Easter-egg hunts long after their child stopped believing in the Easter Bunny, returning to vacation spots that they went to as children, and participating in Saint Patrick's Day parades. Often, traditions passed down across generations hold special meaning for a family but may not be detected as such by an outsider. This father recounted carrying on the tradition of going out for breakfast on the weekends.

> On weekends my Dad would take me out on Saturday mornings. That was our alone time for the week, and we would go and have breakfast together. I feel it is really important for each of the kids at least occasionally to have alone time with me. The kids call it "having a date with Dad." It doesn't happen every weekend but I think it is important. Last time I went out with Brian he got all dressed up with a tie and everything, and he took me out with his dollar.

Patterned family interactions are the least deliberately planned and least consciously executed. These can include the type of greeting made when someone returns home, a bedtime prayer, and mealtimes. We have already examined at length the multilayered nature of family mealtimes as one class of patterned family interactions with ritual meaning. The remainder of the book will consider other regular interactions, such as bedtime and getting ready for school, that can be classified as family routines and rituals.

Summary

There is an intuitive appeal to the study of family routines and rituals. The reader can no doubt recall such occasions that were either sources of joy or seemed painful in their tedium. There are several possible entry points to this topic ranging from a focus on specific types of practices to cultural customs and rites. The focus of this book is on how routines and rituals provide a window into the intersection between whole family process and individual development and adjustment. This is a complex enterprise as we must consider both directly observed behaviors mostly commonly reflected in routines as well as indirectly inferred symbolic meanings embedded in rituals. To set the frame for this exploration, we must recognize that families are ever changing systems. They incorporate new members, mourn the loss of members, and blend the heritage of different lineages. In the stream of everyday events families provide structure and order that supports the health and growth of its individual members. Yet, in order for individuals to be healthy they must also be autonomous and possess their own identity. The challenge for family researchers is to identify how the family, as a whole, supports the growth and development of the individual and how the individual, in turn, affects the functioning of the group. This process occurs in a cultural context such that family behavior is simultaneously uniquely its own as well as part of a broader system.

Commonplace events such as mealtimes, bedtimes, and everyday conversations contain routine and ritual elements. Whereas the repetitive structure of routines serves to provide order to family life, the symbolic meaning of family rituals serves to provide emotional connections. As will be examined in the remainder of this book, routines and rituals have the potential to promote as well as disrupt individual health and wellbeing. On a daily basis and across the lifespan, families must continually balance the need to provide organization and structure and emotional connections with shifting needs of the individual. We can directly observe the fine-tuned nature of this balancing act in such settings as mealtimes. Social interactions are regulated to minimize disruptions through attention to manners, setting limits on bouts of conflict, and even cultural standards of acceptable movements away from the table. Topics of conversation at the table may serve to reinforce feelings of belonging to the group by raising sensitive issues such as fear of monsters or "being weird," aligning relationships between parents and child, or just knowing that others will be there for you. I will examine the developmental course, cultural variations, protective functions, and therapeutic use of routines and rituals. I conclude with considerations of the place of routines and rituals in theories of the family context of child development. To begin, I will turn to some of the myths and misconceptions about routines and rituals in contemporary family life.

2

Myths and Misconceptions about Family Routines and Rituals

When I was growing up, my parents both worked, so when we came home from school we'd start dinner and start setting the table, and then when my dad came home, we all sat down to dinner. We had the whole family at the table. It was usually between five and six every night. My father liked everyone to be quiet until after we ate. And then once the food came out, it was like a ritual. You know, we sat down, ate our meal, and then once everyone relaxed, everyone sat around and talked.

Now, it is a little more flexible; we try to eat between five and seven, and sometimes my husband is home late, and it may just be something that I throw together. We all sit down at the table in the kitchen. My son really likes to hold onto the traditions, and my daughter is starting to show an interest. She sees a lot of her friends don't get together as families. She appreciates it now, and she has started to learn from these traditional values.

(Parent of school-aged children)

There is no question that family life in the twenty-first century is marked by busy schedules, multiple demands, and at times a sense of urgency to get the most done. There are also changes in the amount of time parents work outside the home, how many adults reside in the home at any given time, and even definitions of what constitutes a family (Teachman, Tedrow, and Crowder, 2000). Often these structural shifts and the amount of time spent in the home have been confused with the belief that the core of family life and its purpose have changed in significant ways (Popenoe, 1993). Take, for example, the increasing rate of employment outside the home among women with young children in the past two decades. To some this change in work patterns suggested that women would no longer be good mothers because they were away from their children for part of the day. Yet the research did not bear out this belief, as working mothers are just as likely to have children who are securely attached, emotionally healthy, and successfully make the transition from home to school (Clarke-Stewart, Gruber, and Fitzgerald, 1994). Similar myths and misperceptions have plagued the study of family routines and rituals. Many of these myths are rooted in televised images of the family, a failure to understand the relatively recent development of rituals as family-based events, and how emotions may influence our perceptions of how much time is actually spent with the family. Let us first examine some of the televised images that illustrate these myths.

Ozzie and Harriet Images of Family Life

Current misconceptions about family life seem to be rooted in images of television families. Perhaps the most notable and regularly referenced example is that of Ozzie and Harriet. To review for those not familiar with the show, *The Adventures of Ozzie and Harriet* was a family situation comedy that aired from 1952 to 1966. The televised images revolved around the adventures of Ozzie (the father), Harriet (the mother), and their two sons, Ricky and David. They lived in relative harmony and faced such dilemmas as whether they should get a new dog or whether David should have his own key to the house. Some have seen these images as a realistic portrayal of family life in the late 1950s. Others have gone so far as to propose that *Ozzie and Harriet* represents core family values tied to the nuclear family. There is a wistful nostalgia associated with these positions such that a particular form of family life (the two-parent suburban household) is considered a prototype of the good life—and one that is quickly slipping away. Yet, as Gregory Curtis writes in the *New York Times Magazine:* "*The Adventures of Ozzie and Harriet* was set in an imaginary small town where there is never any politics, any contention, any heartbreak. Everyone is happy. Everyone is well fed and well dressed, lives in a nice house and has the same heart and the same values" (Curtis, 1997, 40). Thus, the prototypical family depicted in *Ozzie and Harriet* never existed. But elements of their lives may resonate with contemporary families. Curtis continues: "Ozzie knew that for a family something as mundane as buying a car or a mother's getting a new hair style is a huge occasion. He knew something else too. The string that ties a family together is spun from a series of minute decisions, of routines, of hellos and goodbyes and hellos again. And there is nothing about these greetings and daily decisions that depends on wealth or class" (41). The importance of daily routines need not be equated with a particular set of values or political rhetoric. Rather, there is a focus on which elements of family organization may be simultaneously preserved across generations as well as adapted to the changing family landscape.

It may not be surprising that televised images of family life hold such sway in our minds when thinking about what constitutes expectable patterns of interaction. Television families are purposely portrayed interacting in commonplace settings, such as the kitchen or living room, doing commonplace activities, such as preparing a meal or reading a newspaper. These scenes are carefully constructed so that they make sense to viewers and resonate with their daily lives. Some commentators on popular culture note a "double decay" of the family in its real existence and its virtual portrayals. Routines allow for the identification of which televised images of family life reflect a deterioration of substance predicting the future course of the family as an institution. The distinction between the homespun wisdoms of the Waltons (a three-generation family with seven children living in Virginia's Blue Ridge Mountains) and the incoherent outbursts of the Simpsons (a cartoon family of five where the father is routinely portrayed as a buffoon) is considered to be a true and valid reflection of the demise of the family as a source of emotional support and positive socialization. Yet, just as women in the workforce did not lead to wild and abandoned children, there does not appear to be a clear and parallel weakening of the family fiber in televised images when images from the mid- to late twentieth century are compared (Douglas, 2003). Although some attention has been paid to how conflict resolution and stability in relationships have changed in television portrayals over the past fifty years, less attention has been paid to how daily routines are managed. In general, daily routines are managed quite well in television families (Douglas, 2003). One study compared televised images of families depicted in the 1950s (*Father Knows Best, My Three Sons*) with those in the 1980s and 1990s (*Family Ties, Roseanne, Home Improvement*) and studied whether couples were able to handle daily routines effectively, coped with day-to-day life, or let "life get on top of them" (Douglas and Olson, 1995). There was a trend for the more contemporary spouses to be less organized and less able to cope with the day-to-day aspects of family life. However, a similar type of content analysis that included sibling and parent-child relationships revealed that most routine tasks were handled effectively (Douglas, 2003). It may be that managing daily life is of more concern to contemporary family members and is thus incorporated into television scripts to keep viewers' attention. It is also the case that content analysis does not allow for an examination of more process- and meaning-laden features associated with ritual elements of family life. However, traditional content analysis of television images of family life does support the portrayal of a group that cares for its members, manages daily challenges relatively effectively, and is fairly stable. Thus, the demise of the family as an organized and nurturing group as evidenced by television images appears to be based largely on preconceived conjectures and nostalgia rather than on an examination of the whole story. A similar argument can be made when we examine the historical roots of family rituals and their role in contemporary family life.

A Century of Change in Family Rituals

Contrary to the notion that family rituals have devolved over time is evidence that these collective gatherings have evolved from the mid-1800s into modern life. During the Victorian era, families consisted of individual members who typically went their own ways. In the early nineteenth century, meals were caught on the run, and family members rarely ate together. Indeed, the dining room as a separate place in the typical family home did not appear until the late 1800s. The family meal as a time set aside for family communication and the expectation for attendance did not develop until the mid-nineteenth century (Caplow, Bahr, Chandwick, Hill, and Williamson, 1982). The word *weekend* did not come into use until the 1880s, and only then could family weekend activities come into being. Even such religious holiday celebrations as Christmas were considered communal rather than family events until the late nineteenth century (Gillis, 1996).

Historians speculate that following the Industrial Revolution, families reorganized their daily lives in accordance with shifting work patterns outside the home. During the day, family members went to work or school, and upon their return home they invented the family dinner, parlor games, and bedtime routines. Thus, in many respects family routines and rituals have evolved to protect the family from being pulled apart by outside influences. JohnGillis, a noted family historian, remarks: "Ritual has come to perform the same compensatory function for families as it once did for communities. And, in this century, we have come to rely more on ritual to provide us with a stable, reassuring family that we can live by even when we are no longer living in stable family relationships" (Gillis 1996, 13). Indeed, the complex nature of child raising in the twenty-first century demands more attention to coordinating activities and extends over a longer life span than in the past (Coontz 2000).

In 1950, sociologists James H. S. Bossard and Eleanor Stoker Boll published their seminal work titled *Rituals in Family Living* (Bossard and Boll 1950). Drawing on interviews, family memorabilia, autobiographies, and case studies, they conclude that family rituals are at the core of family life. This is not to suggest that the organization of family rituals has not changed with time. Bossard and Boll identified seven ways in which rituals changed from the beginning of the twentieth century until the late 1940s. First, ritual practices moved from predominantly religious to secular activities. Even rituals associated with such religious observances as Christmas moved into the home. Second, rituals shifted from large-group to small-group gatherings. This was no doubt due to changes in living arrangements and distance between family members. The home came to be viewed as a retreat from the social world and as organized around the needs of children. Creating private spaces and activities was characteristic of modern families, in contrast to family life's being organized around productivity and economic survival (Hareven, 1985).

The third alteration was the practice of family rituals within a stable to a more mobile group. Even with a more mobile society, families find ways to preserve their connections to the past. A relatively common feature of many households is the presence of plates and dishes that have been passed down across generations. In 15 percent of families interviewed in Chicago, eating utensils were identified as special objects they had inherited that deserved designated places in the home (Csikszentmihalyi and Rochberg-Halton, 1981). As one respondent recounted, "Well the most important things would be the pewter mugs which have been in my family since the 1700s. They are things that I inherited from my mother, who just passed away. [Without them] I think part of my family tradition would be missing. I intend to carry that forward" (83).

The next three changes are pertinent to our discussion and highlight how family rituals may be a logical consequence of the pressures faced by contemporary families. During the late nineteenth century and into the twentieth century, the family became more child-centered, shifted from a communal family ideology to a democratic one, and changed from a community-integrated to an individualized group. Let us examine each point in turn as it relates to the practice of family rituals. Most historians agree that the shift from an adult-centered to child-centered family marked a significant change in how the group functioned. Family roles became more clearly demarcated, particularly for female members of the household. Once work became separated from home life, division of labor included not only specific jobs within the household but also the assignment of roles that became associated with family definitions (women in middle-class families took on the role of "mother" and working-class women took on the role of "child care provider"). Activities focused on care for the young, and women thus became in charge of the rhythms of the day. This can be seen as restricting the role that women play in the broader social and political culture. Indeed, the division of household work is considered an essential element in understanding gender in the family (Coltrane, 2000). What this division portends for the study of routines and rituals is that women are often considered the "kin keepers" of the family (Leach and Braithwaite, 1996; Oliveri and Reiss, 1987). That is, women take on the role of keeping track of other family members, establishing lines of communication, and congregating members.

The shift from a communal to a democratic definition of family paved the way for multiple voices to be heard in constructing family rituals. No longer the dictum of the stalwart elder male (or the king), family rituals were created in a way that reflected the wishes and desires of all family members. Halfway through the twentieth century, family councils as regularly set times for family problem solving were recommended as ways of effectively handling problematic behaviors (Dreikurs, 1948). Interestingly, these meetings were designed to reinforce a sense of equality among family members (Dreikurs, Gould, and Corsini, 1974).

The shift from a socially to an individually regulated group created an opportunity for each family to develop its own unique rituals and routines. Indeed, this is the mark of contemporary rituals, whereby each family comes to define what constitutes a ritual for them. For some families, this may be a special meal once a week; for others, a Saturday outing with the dogs. The individualized nature of the contemporary family allows for unique and varied interpretations of what counts as a ritual.

The seventh shift that Bossard and Boll noted was the move from a neighborhood-enclosed family to one isolated in an urban environment. Certainly this characteristic rings true for families in the twenty-first century. This shift, in essence, places the burden of routine management into the hands of single households rather than relying on cooperation among extended family members who may live within walking distance of one another (Hareven 1985).

Bossard and Boll argue that as family organization and structure shifted from the late 1800s into the mid-twentieth century that there were *more* rather than *fewer* opportunities to gather as a family. They identify twelve areas where these changes were most prominent in *their* studies.

1. Educational practices. As education moved from home-based to more formalized settings, new rituals needed to be developed such that time was set aside for homework and study was delegated as an after-school activity. Dinnertime also changed to accommodate children returning from school rather than being served at the middle of the day.

2. Reading rituals. During the early 1800s, reading out loud as a group was common. With the advent of formalized education, group reading was replaced with setting aside time for individual reading, and for younger readers, joint book reading with a parent or older sibling became more common.

3. Saturday night baths. In agrarian culture, the Saturday night bath was a necessity linked to preparation for the Sunday service. The Saturday night bath ritual was retained, and access to and time allowed in the bathroom were ordered by age and work status.

4. The Sunday drive. During the days of horse and carriage, the Sunday drive was considered a source of family pride, with horses especially groomed and the family well washed. It was a time for show and comparison with one's neighbors. More contemporary Sunday drives are seen as an escape from the week's routine, seeing new sights, and having relaxing fun.

5. Home entertainment. Isolated from neighbors, the family became the seat of diversion. During the late 1800s to the mid-twentieth century, families organized musical evenings, family plays, spelling bees, and family-invented games. Bossard and Boll note that in the late 1940s the advent of Sunday night radio shows provided additional opportunities for the family to share time.

6. The evening snack. Bossard and Boll note that a "fourth family meal" was often shared between adolescents and their parents. This time was set aside for solving problems, getting something off one's chest before retiring, and giving advice. In families with different work shifts, this

may be one of the regular times that multiple members are home at the same time.

7. Doing the dishes. For more privileged families this may have signified a change from employing full-time live-in servants.

8. Walking the dog. Once there was no longer a barn or wide outdoors to house the family dog, someone needed to be responsible for its care. These duties are often assigned to children once they reach an age of responsibility.

9. Present-giving. The exchange of gifts at holidays and birthdays developed. Ties between individuals are often revealed in gift-giving, with gifts to the closest kin being the most valuable (Cheal, 1988a). Sociologists speculate that gift-giving among family members becomes an increasingly important ritual as demands and threats to family social ties increase (Caplow, 1982).

10. The family meal. The advent of markets, refrigeration, and the move away from farm-based family life resulted in preserving dinnertime as the occasion when all the family could be together and catch up on the day's events. Also during this time, particular meals during the week were identified as special set-aside times, such as Sunday breakfast and once-a-week outings to a restaurant.

11. Community-provided rituals. These might include movie night, visits to local fairs, or seeing the department-store Santa.

12. Father-child ritual schedules. With being away from home during most of the day, fathers created scheduled times to be with their family. This may range from play-time with infants when returning home from work, Saturday recreational outings, and help at homework time.

Unfortunately, we have little reliable data that can directly compare contemporary family activities with those in the 1950s. Anecdotally, we note that several of these activities were described in interviews we conducted with families in the 1990s.

Family Chores

It's very similar in my house as it was growing up. My sister and I were in charge of setting and clearing the table. Now Caroline sets the table, and we all kind of clear together. Junior is in charge of walking the dog every morning before he goes somewhere, and Sally is a little bit young to do chores. She helps me with the garden, but she's only five. And they all are responsible for picking up their rooms and their toys and their books.

Sundays

Then on Sunday morning we go to church at 9:30, so everybody's up and they eat breakfast before they go to church. We get back from church and Sunday school at about noon. Most Sundays, we have family activities, like we don't do any chores around the house or errands so much on Sundays. We visit grandparents or visiting aunts and uncles and cousin or family friends. Sometimes we have people over for dinner or go to somebody else's house for dinner. Sometimes we go for a hike, ice-skating, or fishing. It's that kind of a family day. Bath nights are Sunday night usually, so we get to prepare baths and watch TV. At 8:30 it's bedtime, and lights out by 9:00.

Community Santas

When I was a little girl my mom would take me to a store downtown, and there were lots of beautiful decorations all over the place. And we would go to the back of the store, and Santa was sitting on a big chair. And we talked about Christmas and about what I wanted to have for Christmas and how happy I was to see Santa, and I was so excited that I almost forgot what to say to him, because it was so exciting. Maybe this Christmas you can go see Santa like

Mommy did when she was a little girl. [Story told to four-year-old son]

This anecdotal evidence may be in contrast to surveys conducted in the last half-century. Evidence taken from national polls conducted from the late 1970s to the late 1990s suggests that families spend fewer mealtimes together, attend fewer religious services together, and spend less time just sitting and talking together (Putnam, 2000). These are statistics that should be taken seriously as well as taken in perspective. There is little question that families may feel pressed for time and that there are multiple threats to family time. To understand how shifts in time spent are related to routines and rituals, it is important to examine the complex issue of family time.

Time and Time Again:
The Duality of Family Time

Just as family rituals evolved during the late nineteenth century, concepts of family time have shifted across the millennium. Families, as a group, did not attend to time until the late nineteenth century, when clocks became part of the household furnishings. The end of the twentieth century and beginning of the twenty-first century was marked by increasing amounts of time spent by parents working outside the home, by children watching television and playing video games, and by the family eating out together (Huston, Wright, Marquis, and Green, 1999). Parent work schedules may affect how much time is available for such family activities as mealtime, church, and social visits (Hofferth and Sandberg, 2001). It is clear that family members are pulled in different directions and that time demands often compete with spending time together as a group. Indeed, a consistent finding in polls conducted over the past ten years is that on average, over 75 percent of families state that they wish they had more time to spend with their families (Snawerdt, 2002), and this sentiment extends to adolescents (Fagan, 2003). Given these dire statistics it is not unreasonable to conclude that family time is not only threatened but close to extinction. However, this may be a premature conclusion based on the notion that family time is linear, objective, and reliably reported.

Talking about Family Time

Sophisticated time-sampling techniques and reliance on the perspective of multiple informants may provide a gross index of how much time families spend in selected activities. However, family time includes not only how much time is spent together but also beliefs about the importance of family time. Gillis points out that the historical study of family time has focused on locating and dating family activities rather than on how families create beliefs about time through their rituals, myths, and stories (Gillis, 1996). As Gillis emphasizes, family time is not objective and universal but is a cultural construction that signifies the families we live by rather than the families we live in.

Family time is also a subjective phenomenon that involves an exploration of beliefs and desires that shape the everyday experiences of family life (Daly, 2001). Based on interviews with parents of young children, three dimensions of family time have been identified: family time is created as a source of memories; it involves togetherness and positive interactions; and it is highly valued when it is spontaneous (Daly, 2001). Thus the notion of family time, often called quality time, is not directly measurable in terms of minutes per day but reflects family beliefs about what is important in maintaining a cohesive group. This presents something of a conundrum as we examine family routines that involve repetitive practices with some sense of order and place in time. We have already noted that family rituals involve perceptions or beliefs about the relative significance of an event. Thus, when we attempt to locate family practices and representations in time, we must simultaneously take into account the frequency or amount of time spent in an activity and the feelings connected to investing time in an endeavor.

If we consider the subjective experiences of family time, then we are able to expand our discussion to include not just the nature of families but also the culture of organizing collective experiences. No doubt the reader can recall family gatherings that seemed interminable (although only lasting an evening), while others seem all too brief (congenial family vacations). There are demarcations between how much time is actually spent in an activity, how much time one is expected to spend on a particular activity, and how much time one wishes he or she had.

When we frame this issue in the context of family time, it is important to consider family as culture. Groups, including families, are regulated by routine practices that are widely shared, provide routes by which individuals become members of the group, and encourage increasing participation by children as they are able to take on more responsibilities (Goodnow, 1997). These practices are imbued with meanings that reflect the mores and values of the group. A sticky issue in examining cultural practices and beliefs is that there are often elements of ambiguity. This ambiguity is particularly evident in verbal expression of values. Pertinent to this discussion is that there may be inherent incongruities in such phrases as "family time" and "quality time." On one hand, they refer to a location and measurable units. On the other hand, they make sense only when considering what they mean to those involved.

A commonly asked question is how much time is necessary for a routine or ritual to have an effect on individual growth and development. Would it be so simple as to be able to answer that question with a single metric? In the previous chapter I noted that family mealtimes last, on average, twenty minutes. A bedtime story lasts less than five minutes. A kiss given upon leaving and returning home may last less than a second. In the case of family routines, the absolute amount of time spent may not be as crucial as its repetition. When these routines are disrupted, it is their absolute absence that is likely noted rather than the decreased amount of time overall. A forgotten bedtime story or morning kiss may be more disruptive than shortened routines. In family rituals, it is likely the anticipation and deliberate planning that adds to the emotional tenor of these gatherings. It may not be that more time is necessarily equated with more symbolic meaning. Indeed, feelings of being overburdened and overextended may actually detract from the potentially positive benefits of rituals. Thus, when we consider how families organize their lives in time, we must take into account not just the absolute amount of time they spend together but also how that time is structured, the repetition of different activities, and the emotional investment made in sustaining such activities.

Summary

I began this chapter with an examination of some myths and misperceptions about family life. We all hold images of what we think family life should be like. Ideally, we want a family that cares for us, provides shelter and economic resources, listens to our problems, and supports us when we are in distress. Often, we turn to popular culture for a validation of what family life could be or is truly like. If we approach popular images with a nostalgic lens and yearning for what we believe was a more ideal and harmonic time for families, then we miss important attributes of the family as an organized system that has evolved to be more adaptive and supportive of individual needs and desires. Many of the historical shifts noted in the evolution of family routines and rituals suggest that families, as a system, have developed to accommodate individuals' ever-increasing involvement in the social world outside the home. This social world is not always as welcoming as the family hearth; family rituals thus developed to protect the family as a unit and to provide refuge from impersonal work environments. Rather than develop in a commercial fashion, family rituals emerged based on the unique characteristics and talents of individuals. The opportunity for families to define for themselves what constitutes a ritual continues to be a defining quality of contemporary practices.

Why is it that we hold onto nostalgic images of family life and often consider family rituals a practice of the past? Perhaps it lies, in part, in the ways that rituals connect us to the past through memories and symbolic objects. We have noted that rituals provide connections between generations and a foundation for emotional lineage. The fact that we hold onto physical objects such as goblets, silverware, and plates that can be used in ritual gatherings suggests that we seek ways to keep the past alive. When we unwrap a serving platter once a year, we are often reminded of those who are no longer with us or perhaps of the gathering the year before. In some cases, these memories are somewhat melancholic with a longing for times gone past. Yet it would be a mistake to confuse these evocative feelings with a deterioration of prevailing practices. Rather, the simultaneous means by which rituals connect us with the past and adapt to the present make them very much still at the core of family life. Let us now turn to how family routines and rituals shift through the family life cycle.

3

Developmental Life Course of Routines and Rituals

Families, like individuals, have a life cycle. The first issue to consider is "What are the different parts of the family life cycle?" Although this may seem to be a relatively straightforward question, it is somewhat complicated because, in most cases, families are composed of at least three generations, each with its own developmental characteristics. There is some consensus, however, that the family life cycle consists of at least the phases of being married (young couple), living with young children, living with adolescents, launching children and moving on, and going through later life (McGoldrick and Carter, 2003). These phases are not always distinct from each other, and indeed families may move in and out of them more than once. For example, divorce and remarriage may result in re-experiencing the phase of being a newly married couple and raising young children simultaneously with raising adolescents. The phenomenon of increasing numbers of college graduates returning home to live with their parents also calls into question whether the nest is ever really empty—or only temporarily vacated.

A second complicating factor in considering the family life cycle is historical and cultural context. The oldest generation's routines and rituals may be distinct from the youngest generation's not only in time but also in place. At the end of the twentieth century, individuals tended to marry at an older age, there were longer periods of cohabitation, and an increasing proportion of households were not composed of two parents living with children, in comparison to the previous generation (Teachman et al., 2000). Furthermore, the increasing ethnic and cultural diversity of contemporary families suggests that many unions will blend cultural heritages in new ways. Whereas these demographic changes may alter the sheer numbers of individuals who can be categorized in any particular stage and configuration at any given time, these shifts do not detract from the importance of considering key transition points in the family life cycle.

The central reason to consider the family life cycle in this book is the importance of how families use routines and rituals during transitions. Family life is marked by a series of transitions often accompanied by a sense of loss and disequilibrium (P. A. Cowan and Cowan, 2003). These transitions do not occur in a day but are often experienced over months or even years. Some parents anticipate their child's making the transition into school or leaving home even before the child's first birthday. Even transitions that have a clear date, such as a wedding, include a preparatory phase that is often marked by increased stress and tension. The family-level uneasiness may be linked to apprehension about the unknown as well as mourning the loss of what was known and comfortable. With each new phase of family life, there is often a redefining of roles, re-evaluation of self, and expansion or contraction of close relationships. Even when the transitional event is eagerly anticipated, such as a wedding or the birth of a child, it can also bring added stresses and strains to the family (Patterson and Garwick, 1994). Family routines and rituals may present opportunities to ease some of the stresses associated with these life cycle transitions as well as show how families develop as organized systems over time (table 3.1).

Something Old, Something New: The Transition from Family of Origin to Family of Procreation

Perhaps one of the most ritualized events of a family life cycle is a wedding. The event itself is replete with roles reserved for this

Table 3.1. Life Cycle Transitions

	Routine	Ritual
Young adulthood	Daily rhythm	Who is invited to family
Early marriage	Financial decisions	celebrations?
		How are old and new blended?
Transition to par-enthood/infancy	Regularity in feeding and eating	Sense of efficacy and compe-tence as an adult
Parenting and preschool	Bedtime, waking, getting dressed	Beginning to make decisions and own family practices
Elementary-school years	Joint book reading Homework	Sense of competence in shared activity Initiate shared activities
Adolescence	Conversations at mealtime Extracurricular routines Peer-based routines	Sense of belonging to a group Linking individual identity to group meaning
Middle adulthood	Coordinating work and home	Investing in family heritage
Older adulthood	Lessening of routine prac-tices and time expectations	Passing on to next generation

occasion—bride, groom, best man, maid of honor, mother of the bride, and so on. The ceremony itself is a highly structured affair that unfolds in a series of symbolic gestures such as "giving the bride away" to another family, assent from the community that the marriage will be supported, and often a symbol of losing virginity and hopes for fertility (breaking glass, throwing rice). The physical symbols and in-cantations may vary by culture and religion. A common thread forms, however, as routines and rituals from two families are now woven into the fabric of the daily lives of the new couple. Some family theo-rists propose that a healthy marriage is predicated on the process of differentiating from the family origin, creating a sense of autonomy (Bowen, 1978), and negotiating how to resolve differences in family-of-origin practices (Wamboldt and Reiss, 1989).

Although weddings are opportunities for bringing families to-gether, they can also be times of exclusion. Weddings can be prob-lematic for gay, lesbian, bisexual, and transgender family members (Oswald, 2000, 2002b). Rather than having their feelings of belonging reinforced, gay and lesbian family members often feel marginalized and are at times deliberately excluded from such family events. Lesbian and gay partners are more likely to be invited to family celebrations when extended family members are aware of the relationship and parents and siblings are supportive (Oswald, 2002a). Thus, the cementing of relationships in a ritualized venue also identifies the valued members of multiple-family sets.

The wedding itself can serve as a marker of role transitions. In a national survey of 572 couples in the Netherlands, the elaborateness of the wedding was dependent on several contextual variables (Kalmijn, 2004). Couples who had not cohabitated, for example, were more likely to have a large and elaborate wedding. Although couples who cohabitate may hold different beliefs about marriage from those of couples who do not, the wedding ceremony reduces uncertainty about taking on a new role. Thus, for couples who have not shared a household, the wedding serves as a symbolic marker of role transitions.

One of the challenges of early marriage is creating a set of daily routines that fit the rhythms of the individuals and determining which rituals will be carried forward from which side of the family. In our interviews we have found that for some families this is a very deliberate process.

> A big tradition in our family is Valentine's Day. When I was growing up we had this huge box that we decorated. About two weeks before Valentine's Day we would mail each other homemade Valentines and bought Valentines. The box would get full. Aunts, uncles, brothers, sisters, mother, father would all send cards. You couldn't open anything until Valentine's Day. Then on Valentine's Day we would have dinner, and then everybody would get their Valentines passed out to them along with little tokens tucked into the Valentine's Day candy. Then we would have a special Valentine's Day cake that my mom had made. It was a really exciting event, and there was a lot of thought and effort that went into it. So when I brought that into our family, my husband thought it was bizarre because he had never heard of anyone celebrating Valentine's Day.

This example illustrates that couples must decide not only how to celebrate a tradition but also which occasions are cause for celebration.

A potential hot topic for newly married couples is the role of religion and the relative agreement or disagreement about its role in ritualized practices. In a questionnaire-based study, we found that couples who shared similar views about the meaning and importance of religious holiday observances were more satisfied in their marriages than couples who held disparate views (Fiese and Tomcho, 2001). Interestingly, this pattern held if couples were of different religious backgrounds or differed in terms of how religious they felt they were. There was a relatively strong link between religious routines experienced in the family of origin and those practiced in the family of procreation. For both husbands and wives, the assignment of roles and the regularity of religious holiday routines experienced growing up were related to routinization of religious practices in their current family. Similarly, when religious rituals held symbolic meaning and were an important part of growing up, couples also reported more connection to their religious rituals in their current relationships.

We know relatively little about how couples go about creating more mundane routines in their daily lives. In a survey of seventy-nine adults and interviews with twenty married couples, seven types of marriage and friendship rituals were identified (Bruess and Pearson, 1997). The rituals that were reported with the greatest frequency were labeled "couple-time rituals." These included enjoyable activities such as sports, hobbies, games, and movies. One couple reported a Tuesday-night bowling ritual, for example. Togetherness rituals were also considered part of couple-time rituals and were characterized by setting aside time to be together as a couple with little regard for the activity, such as Sunday-morning coffee time. A third aspect of couple-time rituals was escape episodes. These rituals were designed to provide an escape from external pressures and often included leaving home for a night or arranging for children to be taken care of for an evening.

Approximately 20 percent of the rituals reported were considered idiosyncratic and symbolic rituals. These might include couple favorites whereby couples identify restaurants, television shows, and foods that they enjoy. One of the symbolic rituals identified was the "private code" ritual. In these instances, couples routinely use nick-names or phrases that hold meaning only for the couple. For example, one couple described a ritual in which whoever brushed their teeth first would put toothpaste on the other's toothbrush. If there had been a disagreement the night before, one spouse might only lay the tube next to the brush, signifying a need to communicate with the other spouse. These examples clearly illustrate how couples create their own unique rituals that become closely tied to their identity as a couple. Interestingly, in this report, celebration rituals were reported as one of the least frequent couple rituals, suggesting that culturally based celebrations, though important, are not uniquely tied to the couple's representation of who they are as a pair.

Daily couple-based routines have also been identified. In a diary study of forty couples, it was found that spouses were in each other's presence, on average, three to four hours a day during the week, and about one hour of this time was in conversation with each other. Couples talked primarily about their children, friends and leisure, economic matters, work, and relationship matters in descending fre-quency (Kirchler, Rodler, Holzl, and Meier, 2001). Conflicts primarily concerned leisure and household expenditures. During the mundane conversations of the day, important decisions are made about how to allocate resources and who is responsible for making decisions. In this study, it was found that joint decision-making was predominant in large purchases for the home (that is, furnishings) and in making leisure and holiday plans. Men were primarily responsible for mak-ing spending decisions on large purchases such as cars, while women were primarily responsible for making purchasing decisions on a daily basis, such as shopping for food. Thus, the routines of household work evolve through daily conversations and allocation of resources.

A unique study linking attachment representations and family rituals in married couples suggests that ritualization may be associ-ated with felt security (Leon and Jacobvitz, 2003). Fifty-two couples were interviewed before the birth of their first child using the Adult Attachment Interview (Main and Goldwyn, 1996). Seven years later, the researchers contacted the families and collected responses to the Family Ritual Questionnaire (Fiese and Kline, 1993). The study found that when both partners were classified as securely attached, they reported more symbolic significance associated with their rituals than when one or both spouses were insecurely attached. Conversely, when both partners were insecurely attached, there was a tendency to be more rigid and inflexible in carrying out family routines. The authors speculate that rigid rituals may provide a sense of predictability to otherwise anxious adults. There may be an emotional cost, however, as the family rituals that were created held little meaning and symbolic significance for these couples. Adults who represented their own caregiving experiences as responsive and reliable and married partners who held similar beliefs were more likely to report meaning and affective commitment to their current family rituals. This is a complicated tale to unravel, as we know little about the course of routine development in these couples nor do we have any information about their relative satisfaction in their martial relationship. The findings of this study do suggest that the relative coherence of relationship representations between couples is related to overall family ritual quality. In other studies, the relative coherence of narratives told about family relationships has been found to be related to marital satisfaction (Dickstein, St. Andre, Sameroff, Seifer, and Schiller, 1999), suggesting that couples create storied representations of their relationships that may include how they engage in rituals.

Perhaps marriage routines and rituals are most telling when they become disrupted following the birth of a child. Let me now turn to how the transition to parenthood is a period of the family life cycle sensitive to changes in routines and rituals.

The Transition to Parenthood

Once the union is formed, the next major alteration in routines typically comes with the birth of the first child. The transition to parenthood is often noted for its challenges to the integrity of the marital relationship as well as increased vulnerability for parental psychological distress (C. P. Cowan and Cowan, 2000). New parents must adapt to and create feeding, bathing, nap-time, and diaper-changing routines. As any new parent will attest, at first the coordination of care can seem overwhelming and unpredictable. One of the many challenges is to create caregiving routines so that they become folded into the stream of daily activities (Lubeck and Chandler, 1990). In a study of 115 families whose oldest child was either an infant or preschool-age, we charted the changes in family routines and rituals (Fiese, Hooker, Kotary, and Schwagler, 1993). Not surprisingly, families whose lives were focused on the intense caregiving demands of raising an infant reported fewer predictable routines and less affect and symbolism associated with family gatherings than parents whose youngest child was of preschool age. We also found that dinnertime routines, weekend activities, and annual celebrations were more regularized in families with preschool-age children than those whose oldest child was an infant (figs. 3.1, 3.2).

Establishing regular routines and predictable rhythms in family life may contribute to parental competence and efficacy. When family and infant routine patterns match, mothers feel more competent and overall family adjustment is more positive (Sprunger, Boyce, and Gaines, 1985). Because of the cross-sectional nature of these reports, we cannot determine whether more competent parenting leads to more predictable routines or vice versa. However, there is evidence to suggest that first-time mothers who have had experience with child-care routines before the birth of their first child may feel more effective as parents (Porter and Hsu, 2003). As new parents engage in daily caregiving activities, they probably also become more confident in their abilities and the routines become more familiar and easier to carry out.

These early caregiving routines provide order and structure as well as encourage social interaction. Take for example, feeding routines established in infancy (Yoos, Kitzman, and Cole, 1999). The adequacy of feeding is affected by three dimensions of routines: temporal anchors, opportunities for social interaction, and biological rhythms. As a temporal anchor, feeding routines evolve based on how frequently the child is hungry and needs sustenance. Breastfed infants typically empty their stomachs within two to three hours, whereas bottle-fed babies usually are hungry every three to four hours. Because feeding occurs on a somewhat regular schedule, there is also the opportunity to link social interaction with the child's needs. When the infant cries for food, the caregiver responds and sets the stage for the child's

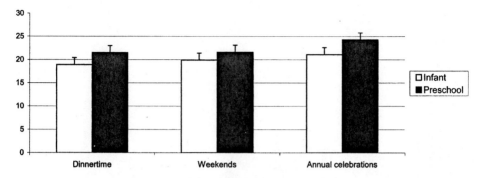

Figure 3.1. Family routine setting differences between early stages of parenthood.

developing awareness of how his or her actions can influence others. Finally, feeding routines are developed within twenty-four-hour blocks and may become aligned with the child's circadian rhythms. There is some evidence to suggest that on-demand feeding routines reinforce the infant's wake-sleep cycle and promote movement into longer nighttime sleeping patterns (Hellbrugge, Lange, Rutenfranz, and Stehr, 1964). Thus, regular routines may promote healthy adaptations in infancy, which in turn may make the infant easier to care for.

Once established, caregiving routines may provide a sense of enjoyment and develop into ritual activities that parent and child eagerly anticipate. Eighty mothers from culturally diverse low-income groups were interviewed about their daily lives (Kubicek, 2002). All the mothers engaged in the regular practice of several routines with their children, including getting dressed, playtime, dinnertime, and bedtime. Some of these routines developed special meaning over time, such as having lunch together on the weekends, going to the library to pick out books, and having Sunday dinner with grandparents. Thus, even at a very young age, children become important players in the development of family rituals.

The creation of meaningful family rituals during this transition period may protect couples from increasing levels of marital dissatisfaction. The transition to parenthood has been noted as a period vulnerable to marital distress (P. A. Cowan, Cowan, Heming, and Miller, 1991). In the previously mentioned study of young parents (Fiese et al., 1993) we found that couples who reported more meaning associated with family rituals were more satisfied with their marital relationship.

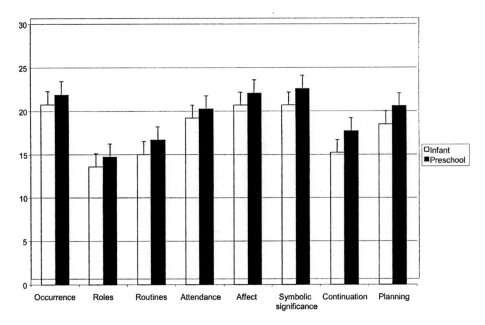

Figure 3.2. Family ritual differences during early stages of parenthood. Scores are summed across routine settings. Occurrence refers to how regularly routine happens; roles refers to assignment of duties during routine; routines refers to regularity of event; attendance refers to expectation for family members to attend event; affect refers to how family members feel during event; symbolic significance refers to whether the event holds special meaning; continuation refers to whether the family plans to carry the tradition into the future; and planning refers to how deliberately the family plans the event.

Specifically, we found that by the time that the oldest child was of preschool age, if parents found little meaning in their family rituals, then they were also less satisfied with their marriages. We do not know if more satisfied marriages lead to more connection through rituals or vice versa. However, the establishment of meaningful rituals during the early stages of parenthood may not only regularize caregiving practices but also be associated with how couples make the transition from partners to parents (C. P. Cowan and Cowan, 2000).

The transition to parenthood is noted by a reorganization of activities to incorporate daily caregiving routines into the stream of daily life. This process evolves over time, taking into account the temperament of the infant and the match between the caregiver and the child's behavior. For some parents this may be an easy transition, whereby previous caregiving experience sets a framework for organizing behavior. In addition, the relative match between parent and infant behavior becomes important. When there is a good match and routines are relatively stable, infants may be easier to soothe, more amenable to daily naps, and less likely to wake in the middle of the night (Sprunger et al., 1985). This predictability, in turn, may reduce parental stress and increase feelings of competence and efficacy.

We can speculate as to how this may unfold as a series of transactions. Parents bring previous experiences that serve as behavioral reference points for caregiving practices (fig. 3.3). These practices are attuned to the child's temperament and geared to fit within the child's and parent's daily rhythms. Routines are then established that may contribute to the infant being able to settle himself or herself and establish regular sleep/wake cycles. With smooth routines in place, the parent may feel competent and equipped to handle the next set of caregiving demands.

Preschool and the Transition to School Routines

During the preschool years, the child becomes a more active participant in the household. In a preliminary report, four classes of child routines were identified: daily living routines (mealtime, bedtime, getting ready in the morning), household responsibilities, discipline routines, and homework routines (Sytsma, Kelley, and Wymer, 2001). Contrary to prediction, discipline routines were not related to child behavior problems. However, daily living routines were negatively related to parents' reports of problem behaviors. Children begin to negotiate with parents about routines during the preschool years. Parents are more likely to make deals with their preschool children around food choice and with their early school-age children about activities (Nucci and Smetana, 1996). Bedtime routines are typically not the subject of compromise during this developmental period. There is also some evidence to suggest that parents experience more fluctuation in their children's daily routines when the children are between two and three years of age than when their child was an infant (Britto, Fuligini, and Brooks-Gunn, 2002). Thus, during the preschool and early elementary years, daily routines call forth negotiation

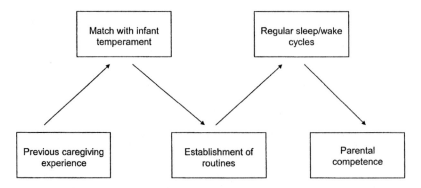

Figure 3.3. Transactional model of caregiving routines.

and shared problem solving. This theme repeats itself during the adolescent years.

The developmental period between three and six years of age is noted for rapid increases in vocabulary and emerging literacy skills. Dinnertime conversations provide repeated opportunities to teach language and expose children to wide-ranging vocabularies (Beals and Snow, 1994; Snow, Dickinson, and Tabors, 1991). I have already discussed some of the effects of dinnertime conversations on children's vocabulary development. I now turn to the specific routines of joint book reading and emerging literacy skills.

Joint book reading between parent and child during the preschool years is consistently related to later language development, literacy skills, and reading achievement (Bus, van IJzendoorn, and Pellegrini, 1995). These effects are linked to the frequency of joint book reading, how parent and child interact during the activity, and parental beliefs about the importance of reading routines. While reading, parents are able to limit distractions and direct the child's attention to key points of the story or picture. Illustrations and repeated story lines, in particular, offer an opportunity for the parent to comment on similarities between the child's experience and actions in the book. Literacy researchers refer to this strategy as "specific commenting," an interaction style found to be related to print awareness and academic success (Hockenberger, Goldstein, and Hass, 1999). The types of comments parents make during joint book reading are often in reference to such routine activities familiar to the child as "Remember when we went to the park?" and "Remember when we went to the grocery store?" Over time, these repetitive reminiscences may contribute to children's understanding of who they are and how they fit into the social world (Fivush, Haden, and Reese, 1996).

Parents' beliefs about the importance of book-reading routines are also associated with how regularly they engage in joint book reading and their child's interest in reading books (DeBaryshe, 1995). Parents who believe that book reading is important and associate it with their child's learning to read, read to their children more frequently and their children ask to be read to more frequently. In this regard, joint book-reading routines involve not only the act of reading but also personal investments to continue the activity over time. As with caregiving routines established during infancy, joint book-reading routines likely are part of a transactional process whereby the child's interest in reading contributes to the parent's engagement in reading and vice versa.

The preschool years are marked by an increasing frequency of routines and child-centered activities. Children who have experienced regular routines and have been part of creating meaningful rituals may be better prepared to meet the challenges of school. The structure of a school day is replete with routines. Getting to school on time, learning to stand in line, and knowing that circle time is at the beginning of the day, naptime is after snack, and Friday is "show and tell" are common routines for a child in kindergarten.

I followed a group of seventy families from the time that one of their children was preschool age into the early elementary school years. I found that family routines at four years of age predicted academic achievement at nine years of age (Fiese, 2000). I also examined whether stability and/or change in family routines and rituals over the five-year period was related to how well the children did in school (Fiese, 2002). Families who maintained a high degree of commitment to their rituals and valued the emotional connections they experienced during their family gatherings over the five-year period had children who scored the highest on tests of academic achievement. Those families whose investment in family rituals remained relatively low over the same period had children who scored the lowest on the standardized tests. Intermediate to these two groups were families who had decreasing meaning in their rituals over the five-year period. These families displayed a commitment to meaningful rituals when their children were four years of age, but the commitment had faded by the time the children reached nine years of age. These children performed intermediate to the other groups and were observed by their teachers as being less socially competent.

Unfortunately, we do not know what other factors, such as added family stress, may have been present during this five-year period and contributed to the results. Similar results, however, have been reported in a sample of low-income single African-American mothers and their elementary school children (Brody and Flor, 1997). For the boys in this sample, family routines were directly related to academic achievement as well as self-regulation. The authors speculate that more routinized homes provided the boys with a sense of control and reduced the likelihood of developing behavior problems incompatible with school success.

One of the challenges during the elementary school years is co-ordinating schedules and assignments between home and school. In interviews of sixty-six families who had a child in either second or third grade, parents were asked about how invested they were in creating homework routines (Serpell, Sonnenschein, Baker, and Ganapathy, 2002). Parents considered doing homework a family activity that involved multiple members. The activity provided an opportunity for parents to monitor their child's development, hear about what was happening at school, and communicate with the teacher. The extent to which homework routines were regularly practiced in the home was related to basic reading skills in the third grade.

Regular routines during the elementary school years may also contribute to better behavioral adjustment. Based on parents' reports, children who engage in more daily living routines (for example, regular bedtime routines, getting ready in the morning) and homework routines are less likely to have behavior problems (Sytsma et al., 2001). In a survey of 2,818 children between birth and age twelve, time spent in family activities, including mealtime, was associated with fewer problem behaviors (Hofferth and Sandberg, 2001). The bulk of data we have to date is correlational, so it is difficult to state with any certainty that the presence of routines leads to better adaptation in the elementary school years. Future research is needed to determine the mechanisms of effect.

In a broader sense, routines must fit with a culture's values and goals (Weisner, 2002). In a literate society success is determined, in part, by being able to read. Joint book reading, setting aside time for homework, and regular communication with the school are examples of routines supported in literate society. Sustained routines provide a stability to family life that promotes health and well-being of its children. I have shown evidence of this in terms of children's performance in school and will return to this point when we consider family health. Routines and rituals do not stop being important at the elementary school years; they continue to have influence during adolescence.

Negotiating Independence and Staying Connected during Adolescence

Adolescence is a time for seeking independence and autonomy from the family. So how may family routines and rituals continue to have influence during this important developmental period? Contrary to the notion that adolescents don't spend time with or need their family some research suggests that shared family time contributes to adolescent adjustment. In a study of 192 dual-earner families with adolescents, the average family spent almost four hours a week in what could be categorized as family time (Crouter, Head, McHale, and Tucker, 2004). Most of this time was spent eating meals together (two hours per week), and 97 percent of the families spent at least some time together over a meal during a seven-day period. Time spent in meals was positively related to parental warmth and marital affection. There was a modest relation between time spent together in meals and less risky behavior by first-born children. In an epidemiological study of 4,746 adolescents, frequency of family meals was associated with better grades and less cigarette, alcohol, and marijuana use (Eisenberg et al., 2004).

These effects are not limited to families residing in the United States. In a survey of 282 adolescents residing in Spain, family celebrations and activities were found to distinguish adolescents referred to a mental-health clinic from those not experiencing emotional distress

(Compan, Moreno, Ruiz, and Pascual, 2002). Adolescents referred for mental-health services reported having fewer meals and holiday celebrations with their parents.

It is possible that greater exposure to family routines affects adolescents much as it does younger children. For example, mealtimes with adolescents may provide opportunities for problem-solving and supportive communication. Family mealtimes during this period may also afford opportunities to learn conflict-negotiation skills (Vuchinich, Emery, and Cassidy, 1988). There is also some indication that teens who do such routine family work as washing the dishes show more concern and care for others (Grusec, Goodnow, and Cohen, 1996).

During adolescence, the relationship between family management strategies and adaptation becomes important. Substantial literature suggests that the more parents monitor adolescents' activities, the better adjusted and academically successful the adolescents will be. One mechanism of this effect is through family management strategies (Furstenberg, Cook, Eccles, Elder, and Sameroff, 1999). Effective parents continue to orchestrate a considerable part of the adolescent's day through coordinating activities and providing support. Indeed, adolescents' reports on family routines have been found to be significantly related to adolescents' total time in constructive activities (Larson, Dworkin, and Gillman, 2001). Family routines may have a direct effect by providing structure and reducing the adolescents' exposure to risky situations. Another way in which family routines may operate during adolescence is the adolescent's perception about his or her parent's emotional investment in family activities. Knowledge of an adolescent's whereabouts also suggests that the parents care for and respect the types of activities that the child is engaged in outside the home.

When parents and adolescents share similar views about the importance of and meaning associated with their family rituals, adolescents have a stronger sense of self and experience less anxiety overall (Fiese, 1992). I suspect that these relations hold for a variety of reasons. When parents and adolescents share similar views about the importance of their family gatherings, there may be overall lower levels of conflict. Conflict may pull family members apart; it has been found that for adolescent girls, conflict in the home was associated with less time mothers and daughters spent eating, watching television, or going somewhere together (Dubas and Gerris, 2002). In addition, fathers' reports of family conflict were associated with fathers spending less time with their adolescent daughters.

The shared meaning and investment in rituals may also provide the adolescent with a sense of belonging to a group. Feelings of alienation, lack of direction, and loneliness may be ameliorated if one has the refuge of a group that engages in expectable and affirming activities. The relation between adolescents' sense of family cohesion and psychosocial maturity may be mediated through their satisfaction with family rituals (Eakers and Walters, 2002). Thus, although the overall amount of time engaged in family routines may decline during adolescence (Larson et al., 2001), the symbolic significance and affective meaning of family rituals remains firm.

Passing Down Rituals and Altering Routines in Older Adults

Older adults often play the role of "kinkeepers" and are responsible for transmitting rituals across generations. The birth of a grandchild can engender interest on the part of grandparents to reintroduce rituals they practiced during their own child-raising years. In one study, 65 percent of grandparents interviewed could identify rituals practiced by their children and grandchildren that had roots in their own caregiving activities (Rosenthal and Marshall, 1988). Family members typically identify the kinkeeper as a female somewhere between the ages of forty and fifty-nine (Leach and Braithwaite, 1996). At some point, however, older adults make the decision that their role as kinkeeper and organizer of family rituals needs to be passed on to the middle generation. The decision to make such a transition may be based on failing health, feeling burdened, or just thinking it was time for someone else to do it.

There may be a decreasing frequency in the practice of routines in older age. Seven women over the age of seventy were interviewed, and it was found that although these women used routines to facilitate their well-being they did so to a lesser extent when they were working or had children living at home (Ludwig, 1998). The decreasing prevalence of routines appeared to be associated with feelings of lessening obligations both inside and outside the home. Some of the respondents noted an imposition when children or grandchildren came to visit because it meant re-implementing routines such as regular mealtimes and waking times.

We know relatively little about how the meaning behind rituals may continue to be important for older adults. However, religious rituals and Thanksgiving are considered the most important rituals to older adults, with regular family activities seen as least important (Meske, Sanders, Meredith, and Abbott, 1994). It may be that, with age, rituals become more circumscribed around cultural and religious venues, with less attention paid to unique family routines.

Rituals of Loss

At the end of the family life cycle, members depart and are remembered through rituals. The most clearly demarked of these gatherings are wakes and funerals. Wakes and funerals generally include predictable order and expectations for attendance. Wakes are often noted for an abundance of food, many of the dishes passed down across generations. Mourning and loss rituals have been described as a form of emotional containment that allows people to experience strong feelings while being supported by caring individuals (Roberts, 2003). Although rituals may be established to provide a sense of belonging and group identity, bereavement rituals may also signify emotional loss.

Just as the transition from one stage of family life to the next may not be clear-cut, instances of ambiguous loss may also affect the family and call for ritual recognition. Ambiguous loss can include such circumstances as miscarriage, abduction, or being held as a prisoner of war where there are no clear cultural guides. At times, there may even be no legal recognition that the individual is gone. Families can also experience ambiguous loss when a loved one is physically present but psychologically absent, as in the case of Alzheimer's disease. In such cases, families experience stress associated with the ambiguity of the situation (Boss, 1999). In the case where a family member is physically absent, a ritualized recognition through a memorial service may ease some of the transitions necessary in confronting that the individual may never return to the family. In the case where the family member is physically present but psychologically absent, expectations for full participation at family ritual gatherings may need to be altered. Both circumstances may include a grieving process not unlike those undergone during wakes and funerals.

Summary

Routines and rituals mark transitions throughout the family life cycle. There appears to be an ebb and flow of routines such that they are established early on in relationships to provide predictability. For young couples, dating routines are demarked by setting aside time for another person. Infant caregiving routines are structured to provide order to the day. School-age children learn to set their alarm and meet the bus on time, and the school day revolves around set times for activities. During adolescence, more time is spent outside the home and there is the juxtaposition of schedules within and without the family. As individuals age, there is a desire to become more flexible and in a sense "give up the clock." Thus, a consideration of the routine aspects of daily life shows a developmental progression of establishing daily schedules within the home, adjusting to schedules outside the home, and then integrating the world of work and school with the routine demands of home. The rhythms of the day are tightly linked to developmental cycles whereby control of time is gradually relinquished to children and eventually commanded by older adults.

The meaning behind family rituals also appears to have a developmental course. Whereas young children may look forward to a visit from Santa or sending Valentines cards to relatives, during adolescence the symbolic meaning associated with family rituals likely begins to emerge. The symbolic representation of family gatherings may allow the adolescent to disengage from daily activities but still retain a feeling of being connected to the larger group. In this regard, the affective and emotional significance of family gatherings may become part of the adolescent's identity and feelings of security. During the early stages of couple formation, symbolic forms of communication develop and help cement the uniqueness of a particular union. The press to pass on rituals becomes evident in older adults as there is a recognition that rituals are meant to be preserved to insure the emotional lineage of the family.

Embedded within these shifts and alterations are overarching principles of how families work as a social system. Family life is wrought with as well as blessed with change. How the family, as a group, negotiates these changes illustrates its overall functioning as a system. Systems theorists refer to such principles as disequilibrium and homeostasis to describe the process by which complex systems respond to change and reorganize to become more efficient working organizations (Sameroff 1995). All complex systems are organized in such a way that there is a sense of order, there are clear boundaries between subsystems, and there are ways for different parts of the subsystems to communicate with each other. During periods of change (which all systems experience), there is a need for open lines of communication while parts of the system are redefined. For families, developmental transitions can be unsettling and stressful and calls for a realignment of roles and routines. Roles are often renegotiated in the context of routines. I noted, for example, that the routines created as husband and wife may need to be renegotiated when taking on the roles of father and mother. Adolescents negotiate when they are expected to be home for dinner or what time they have to be home on the weekends. These role negotiations also signify redefinitions of self and self in relation to others, another developmental landmark. Couple rituals may define the "we-ness" uniquely created by the pair. With age, definition of self in relation to others through rituals may be less connected to the marital dyad and more closely felt in religious and cultural celebrations as noted with older adults. The point is that developmental transitions provide opportunities, as well as challenges, to negotiate routines and create meaningful rituals that can enrich family life.

Thus far, I have considered how routines and rituals naturally develop and are part of basic developmental processes. I now move to how family routines and rituals vary across some cultural settings.

4

Cultural Variations

Given the careful attention anthropologists have paid to ritual theory and practice in communities around the world, it seems logical to consider cultural variations in family routines and rituals. As discussed in the first chapter, however, my focus is on how routines and rituals may be related to socialization practices and individual health and well-being rather than on mores and customs that may be distinguishable across groups. In this chapter I consider how variations in routine practices reflect the family's role in imparting values and socializing members to be active participants in particular societies. Specifically, I focus on cultural variations in patterned routine interactions at the dinner table, cultural influences on rites-of-passage rituals, and the effects of immigration on family practices. I conclude by examining how extended-kin networks help support individual development in African-American families. Each one of these situations provides opportunities for socialization as well as opportunities for mismatches between the strivings of the individual and the values of the predominant culture. First I consider, briefly, the general domains in which routines and rituals may exert their influence in supporting cultural socialization practices.

Cultures, in general, are organized around sets of principles that guide individuals' behavior such that they are consistent with the mores of the larger society. Cultures vary in terms of the relative value given to individual strivings for autonomy and independence versus the needs of the group (Markus and Kitayama 1994). Related to these values of individualism and collectivism are variations in terms of deference to authority and when individuals are deemed mature enough to make their own decisions. In terms of family organization, these values can affect such important decisions as when to move out of the house or whom to marry.

Cultural values are evidenced in what counts as a personal transgression. In some cultures, for example, a child is more likely to get into trouble for something that could cause shame to the family, while in other cultures punishment is doled out for not understanding that personal actions may cause emotional distress to others (Miller, Wiley, Fung, and Liang 1997). Relevant to our discussion is the notion that interactions in routine settings will be regulated by cultural expectations for desirable behavior.

These values are transmitted, in part, through the organization of daily family life. The study of everyday tasks and situations not only is embedded in culture but also is at the heart and soul of how behavior is shaped by society (Goodnow 2002). By focusing on how families in different cultures carry out daily routines such as household chores, one can get a glimpse at what is culturally relevant and how roles are assigned to facilitate socialization. As Goodnow states, "This is no empty practice" (242). The mundane activities of daily life can reveal how social values, mores, and virtues are expressed and supported in customs.

In examining cultural variations, I am also interested in mismatches between the predominant society and families or between family members and individuals. A mismatch in values presents an added tension for the individual and family members, thus potentially compromises health and well-being. One such situation is a mismatch of values between generations during immigration. A breakdown or deterioration of routines and rituals may indicate difficulties making the transition from one culture to another. Replacing old rituals with new ones, on the other hand, may also be an indication of adaptation to a new cultural environment.

Thus, my consideration of family routines and rituals in cultural context is primarily aimed at examining how such variations support socialization into a society. I also consider how routines and rituals provide a meaningful bridge between cultures. The dinner table is one setting that reveals these socialization practices.

Variations in Daily Patterned Interactions

Even before a child learns to talk, the structure of mealtime may reinforce cultural values. There is considerable variation across cultures in the use of high chairs for feeding infants. In some cultures, most notably Western cultures, high chairs are commonplace and have evolved into complex pieces of furniture. In other cultures, infants are either held in the caregiver's lap to be fed or passed from one person to another throughout the meal. For example, Anglo mothers are more likely than Puerto Rican mothers to feed their infants in a high chair and encourage the infant to feed himself or herself (Harwood, Miller, Carlson, and Leyendecker 2002). Puerto Rican mothers, on the other hand, are more likely to hold their infants on their laps while feeding and are less likely to provide verbal directions during feeding times. Puerto Rican mothers are also more likely than their Anglo counterparts to expect their infants to exhibit what is considered proper demeanor or show respect, cooperate, and be accepted by the larger community. Thus, from the very earliest encounters mealtime interactions are organized in such a way to support practices associated with individualism (self-feeding) or collectivism (proper demeanor). These values are more strongly reinforced in mealtime conversations.

An analysis of the discourse at the table is based on the assumption that patterns of language use are rooted in cultural and social systems. In the introduction to her book *Dinner Talk,* Shoshana Blum-Kulka alerts us to the multi-layered meanings of table talk: "Even the most mundane instances of face-to-face interaction are complex social performances and social meanings are jointly and dynamically negotiated rather than static and individual" (Blum-Kulka 1997, 2).

Blum-Kulka gives a detailed account of mealtime conversations recorded in the households of families living in Jerusalem or the United States. The families fell into one of three college-educated middle- to upper-middle-class groups: Israelis, American-Israeli families living in Israel for more than nine years, and Jewish-American families living in the United States. All of the families had at least two school-age children. Across all groups, adults tended to dominate the conversation. However, there was some variation across the groups in terms of average number of utterances made by children. The Jewish-American children talked the most of the three groups, uttering, on average, forty-eight words in a twenty-minute period. The Israeli children spoke the least, averaging twenty-seven utterances per twenty-minute meal. Not only did the Jewish-American children talk more overall, but they also were more likely to initiate telling a story about an event or activity that occurred on that day than the Israeli children. The stories the Jewish-American children told tended to be "today" stories rather than stories about events that happened in the recent or distant past. These were typically stories told about what happened in school or some other setting away from home.

This focus on daily events in American families has been noted in other comparative studies. One comparison of mealtime conversations of Caucasian and Japanese-American families residing in Hawaii found that Caucasian children were more likely to be asked to talk about an event that happened that day (Martini 1996). Caucasian parents were also more likely to report on their days than Japanese-American parents. Japanese-American families were more likely to talk about a past event that they had shared together. Caucasian parents often used dinner conversation as an opportunity to teach: providing names of dinosaurs, describing the composition of the solar system, and explaining how everyday things work. Japanese-American parents, by contrast, were more likely to include children in conversations about such future family events as vacations or weekend activities.

Cultural distinctions are also found in comparisons between cultures that differ in more subtle ways. One study compared dinnertime conversations between families from the U.S. and from Norway (Aukrust and Snow 1998). Although both countries have been characterized as supporting individualism, Norwegian culture is considered

more homogenous and blends elements of collectivism and individualism. The authors, drawing upon Norwegian scholars, propose that
Norwegian culture can be characterized by values of "local belongingness and equality." Examination of mealtime conversations showed
several similarities between the American and Norwegian families in
terms of child-centeredness and how engaged the children were in
the conversations. The most notable difference between the groups
was in elaboration of social practices. Although all families directed
talk about social practices, the American families were more likely to
converse about behavior of one of the children or internal emotional
states. The Norwegian families were more likely to discuss social practices in the context of broader social institutions. One set of Norwegian explanations had to do with a preschooler's knowledge of what
happens when one doesn't go to work, and the mother explains how
it is possible to get money when unemployed: "It has to do with our
rights. . . . Those who do not work, they can get something called
public assistance." (231).

In these dinnertime observations, a consistent theme emerges
for middle-class Western families. Contemporary American families
are often referred to as child-centered (Bornstein, Tal, and Tamis-
LeMonda 1991). Dinnertime conversations reinforce this value, with
parents encouraging children to be active participants. Routine asking,
"What happened to you today?" contributes to cultural socialization
in at least two ways. Within the larger cultural realm of middle-class
Western families is a value for personal success and individual accom-
plishment (Markus and Kitayama 1994). Asking children (and adults)
to recount their daily experiences provides an opportunity to under-
score expectations for achievement. For example, such innocuous cues
as "How did you do on your test today?"; "Tell Daddy what happened
in gym today"; and "Did you get your homework assignment?" are
embedded in values for individual success. Interestingly, Eastern and
Western cultures differ in terms of attention paid to personal transgressions (Martini 1996; Miller et al. 1997). To simplify a fairly complex issue, in cultures where the community good is highly valued,
personal transgressions are typically cast in relation to violations of
codes of normative conduct, such as "losing face" or causing shame
for the family. In cultures where individual qualities are more highly

valued, personal transgressions are more likely to be framed in light of harm done to a person's feelings. Parents in Chicago may make light of a child's misconduct at the dinner table if it shows off his strong will and independent nature, but the same behavior in Taipei may call forth harsh comments from multiple members of the family.

Dinnertime conversations are also embedded in systems of cultural regulation on a second level. As pointed out in Chapter 1, mealtimes provide an opportunity to reinforce how families may also be distinct from each other. Viewing this process as part of the cultural context shows that family belief systems may regulate the conversation in accordance with family-level as well as cultural boundaries. It is as if a cultural map lays out the landscape of acceptable topics and emotions displayed during routine gatherings. The borders may be dictated by culture. Variations across the landscape, however, are set by characteristics of the family discussed in previous chapters. Topics of discussion at the table may vary from family to family. However, the relative weight given to particular aspects of a topic may be regulated by the predominant culture. Parents in Chicago may tell "hell-raising" stories of their childhood or recount the time their four-year-old backed the car in the garage (Miller, Sandel, Liang, and Fung 2001). Parents in Taipei may tell a story over and over again that highlights their child's greediness for wanting to ride a mechanical car at the market and showing disregard for her aunt's generosity (Miller, Fung, and Mintz 1996). Daily routines such as mealtime gatherings are embedded in cultural practices not only for the foods being served but also as opportunities to reinforce personal and collective values.

Whereas cultural variations may be somewhat subtle when considering daily patterned interactions at the dinner table, rites-of-passage rituals have more distinct and apparent characteristics across ethnic and religious groups.

Rites-of-Passage Rituals across Cultures and Religious Groups

The designation of becoming an adult is a developmental task that extends across cultures. In some cultures there is a clear-cut distinction such that after a public ceremony, the child earns all the rights and privileges of an adult. It is beyond the scope of this book to address how rites-of-passage rituals signify cultural beliefs about maturity and responsible contributions to society. Rather, I will focus on two coming-of-age" rituals that reflect family connections among three generations as well as adaptations that need to be made to accommodate the contemporary position of the youngest generation. The first rite to consider is the Bar Mitzvah, and the second is the celebration of girls' fifteenth birthdays in Mexico.

Family Continuity and the Bar Mitzvah

The Bar Mitzvah dates to as far back as the fifteenth century if not the eighth century. The Bar Mitzvah is a ceremony that coincides with a boy's thirteenth birthday and marks his obtainment of religious majority. Bat Mitzvahs, celebrations for thirteen-year-old girls, were first instituted in the 1920s and became more widely practiced in the 1970s. Although there is not a large literature describing the ceremonies' influence on families and families' preparation of the ceremonies, there are case reports of families as they prepare for, engage in, and reflect upon Bar Mitzvahs (Davis 2003). On one level, the Bar Mitzvah ceremony is orchestrated to highlight the youth's emerging maturity. Preparing a speech, learning the *haftorah,* and dancing with the elders place the youth clearly at the center of attention for this celebratory event. However, the passage is as much for the entire family as it is for the thirteen-year-old. Preparing for the celebration often demands negotiations and compromises between generations. In one case report, this meant a careful examination of how to include the new wife of the child's divorced father. For another family, this meant reconciling differences with a grandparent. The case reports showed throughout that the developmental transition reinforced autonomy for the youth but also brought into relief multigenerational connectedness. The ceremony itself is a consecrated rite for the individual. The meaning behind the ceremony, however, is one of family identity and balance between individual autonomy and family belongingness. Thus, during times of developmental transitions, multiple family members are involved and these are often times for redefining roles and self in relation to others.

Becoming a *Mujercita:* Celebrating
a Girl's Fifteenth Birthday in Mexico

The celebration of a girl's fifteenth birthday in Mexico consists of a Mass to give "gracias a Dios" (thanks to God) and a fiesta. Initially celebrated by those of wealth and high family status, the event has become more predominant in lower-income families. Before the celebration, most girls attend a catechism class led by a female member of the church. Much of the discussion in the class revolves around psychological and physical changes that the girls are experiencing. A portion of the class is dedicated to a discussion of ancestral links to the Aztec warriors and affirmation that generations before the daughter had engaged in this ceremony, which was often a precursor to marriage and reproduction for the good of the community. Over a period of eighteen months, a group of families were observed in Guadalajara preparing for and engaging in the celebrations (Napolitano 1997). The Mass itself resembles a wedding, with the girl being escorted into the church by her godfather and leaving the church with her *chambelano* (male chaperone). Rather than increasing the girl's autonomy, the ritual signifies expectations for greater family control and responsibilities for the daughter. At this point, the girl is seen as a potential bride and the ceremony is a thinly veiled assurance of her virginity. As she becomes "eligible" through the ceremony, her parents must put greater restrictions on her relationships with boys. More careful control by the parents often translates into more housework for the daughter and a lessening of physical affection between daughter and father. Thus, the ritual is a sign of changing relationships within the family in preparation of the daughter leaving home to establish her own family. Interestingly, the ritual itself is practiced less often in Mexico now in families of higher social status. Although the fiesta originated with families who could afford elaborate celebrations, contemporary families with notable wealth are more likely to deride such rituals. In this light, the ritual is seen as archaic and does not take into account the role that women may take on as students and professionals. In contrast, this tradition tends to be preserved in Mexican-American families and has become an affair of quite grand proportion for some families in Miami (Falicov 2001). Thus, this ritual may reflect not only how families respond to cultural and economic changes but also the importance of preserving country-of-origin rituals following immigration.

If we consider the Bar Mitzvah and the celebrations associated with becoming a Mujercita as family rituals, we can identify elements of each that support cultural values of what it means to be an adult in a family. In the case of the Bar Mitzvah, the young man takes on new public roles that are witnessed and celebrated by his family. The roles within the family become realigned to accommodate a new mature member, yet the unity of the family is maintained and reinforced. The underlying meaning is that of family strengths and enduring bonds across generations. In the case of the celebrations for the Mujercita, passage into adulthood indicates the initial preparations for marriage. The ritual itself is replete with symbolism linked to sexual unions. Family roles also shift. In this case, however, the patriarchal role of the father is reinforced as he prepares to receive suitors for his daughter. This rite of passage returns the daughter to the fold of the family prior to her marriage. Although the meaning behind these rites-of-passage rituals may be different, they both tighten family bonds within the boundaries of the culture.

Immigration and Family Ritual Transformations

Migration to a new country can present a host of challenges in maintaining family rituals. A distinction can be made between "both/and" solutions and "either/or" choices when families face dilemmas following migration (Falicov 2003). "Either/or" choices suggest that families must favor one culture over another, with the implicit assumption that the practice that is rejected is associated with a culture of lesser value or significance. The "both/and" solution rests on the assumption that families can blend different traditions and alternate practices depending on context rather than living between two worlds. Family therapists note that transitions that do not include the public display of rituals, as in the case of divorce, homosexual unions, and a handicapped adult member leaving home, set the stage for unresolved loss (Imber-Black 2003). A similar situation is evident in families who experience migration. Although preparing for migration may involve attention to many family-level symbols, they are often "packed away." It is not atypical for families to carefully wrap family photos, select small pieces of cloth woven in their community, or fill vials with native soil in preparation for the move. Once they have arrived at their new home, the question becomes how these symbolic representations of cultural roots will be incorporated into the new setting.

When balancing the need to maintain old traditions while becoming part of a new culture, families may spontaneously create four types of rituals (Falicov 2003). Rituals of connection allow the family to maintain contact with their country of origin. This may take the form of an annual return to the homeland for reunions or special holidays, or routine trips to the post office to send money to extended-family members who have not migrated. The planning, regularity, and communication involved in transferring money across two countries can "have the same psychological effects as the Sunday visit to one's elderly parents nearby" (292).

Re-creation rituals involve structuring space in a way that is familiar and comforting. At the most basic level this may mean living in a neighborhood where other families from the home country live, opening an ethnic restaurant, or attending weekly markets. Attention to smells, sounds, colors, and tastes predominate re-creation rituals as there is an attempt to make daily experiences as genuine as possible.

Memory rituals involve storytelling about past experiences. For some families, there may be a detailed and elaborate migration story. The content of the story provides details about the circumstances of migration, reflections on the good and bad aspects of the homeland, and who was left behind. The process of telling the story allows the family an opportunity to process and evaluate their place in their new country. The creation of a coherent account of the migration process may be associated with resilience and connections to the new country (Cohler 1991).

The fourth type of migration ritual is preserving culturally patterned rituals. These rituals range from culturally prescribed rites of passage to such daily routines as the type of grace that is said before a meal. One way families often maintain connections to their cultural origins is the practice of folk medicine (Pachter, Cloutier, and Bernstein 1996).

Whereas family therapists have identified the different ways in which rituals can be preserved following immigration, researchers have examined how beliefs and values tied to particular cultures are reinforced in family routines for immigrant children. Traditional Chinese culture dictates that the needs of the larger group take precedence over individual desires. The family expresses this widely held belief in expectations that children will respect their elder's wishes and that family obligations have priority over individual wishes. Chinese adolescents in America can feel pulled in opposite directions as the family expects the adolescent to fulfill household obligations and their friends expect them to participate in peer-group activities. Using a daily diary approach, 140 adolescents of Chinese immigrant parents were asked to keep track of their daily activities and feelings over a two-week period (Fuligini, Yip, and Tseng 2002). The most common family activity reported was eating a meal, followed by spending leisure time and engaging in household chores. On average, the adolescents reported two family obligation activities per day and spent slightly more than an hour each day assisting and being with their families. Overall, girls spent more time and carried out more family obligations than did boys. Socializing with peers was negatively related to family obligations on any given day. However, the amount of time spent in family obligations did not necessarily lead to greater conflict or personal distress for these adolescents. These youths appear to expect to balance family and social obligations and make deliberate decisions to spend time with their families. Rather than leading to a sense of alienation from peers, these daily practices may reinforce cultural beliefs and provide a sense of identity. The report stated, "Family obligations may provide the children from immigrant families with a sense of identity and purpose in an American society that, at times, has been accused of emphasizing individualism at the cost of heightened adolescent alienation" (311). Thus, individual identity created in the family is also regulated by cultural mores.

Extended-Kin Networks

Families vary in terms of the degree to which they actively rely on networks of extended kin. African-American families are significantly more likely than whites to call upon extended kin and to live in a community that links several households (Taylor 2000). Anthropologists and sociologists propose that this form of family structure evolved from family traditions of West African cultures (Sudarkasa 1988). There is a complex story to be told about the changing nature of the extended family in response to economic pressures and societal changes. This is a story beyond the scope of this chapter. However, the ways in which extended-family members can act as sources of social support and affect the course of daily routines has gained some empirical support and is pertinent to our discussion.

There is some variation by cultural heritage as to whether extended-kin assistance is seen as desirable. African-American, Mexican-American, and Anglo-American mothers were interviewed about using extended kin in assisting with childcare (Uttal 1999). Whereas African-American and Mexican-American mothers considered extended-kin care as an appropriate practice, Anglo-American mothers described extended-kin care as undesirable even though they relied on it as a backup. The author speculates that the differences in acceptability of relying on extended kin reinforce cultural values of family obligations and responsibilities. For some African-American and Mexican-American families, family responsibilities extend beyond a single household and extended kin expect to be called upon for assistance.

Among Latino families, there is a deep sense of familism expressed through feelings of obligation, solidarity, and interdependence among family members (Cauce and Domenech-Rodriquez 2002). It is not unusual for grandmothers to be actively involved in the care of their grandchildren and to reside in the same home as their daughters. Whereas this arrangement may be seen as intrusive for Anglo Americans, it is considered supportive and associated with more positive parenting behaviors in young Puerto Rican mothers (Contreras 2004). In this regard, assistance with daily chores and child care can be seen as helpful or meddling, depending on how the culture values support from other family members. Assistance from others is not limited to child-care duties.

In a series of studies of African-American adolescents, researchers examined the role of extended-kin social support and effects on family organization on individual adjustment (R. D. Taylor 1996; R. D. Taylor and Roberts 1995). Consistent with previous reports, adolescent psychological functioning and academic performance was directly associated with family organization around set routines and schedules. Kinship support, as perceived by the adolescent, was not directly related to adolescent outcome but was associated with family organization. Thus the effect of kinship support was mediated, in part, by family routines.

Kinship support may enhance parenting practices, and families that are highly organized may attract more support from extended kin. Cultural context, however, tempers the desirability of social support. Thus, it is possible that the acceptance of kinship assistance may be part of a transactional process whereby support may lead to greater ease in creating routines and routines in turn provide a structure to engage extended family members into daily exchanges, depending on the cultural context in which the support is offered. In some cultures, social support is seen as part of the natural order of daily life. In other cultures, however, family boundaries are more distinct and offers of assistance in daily chores, even when needed, are perceived as intrusive rather than helpful. We should also recognize that kinship support is offered in an economic as well as cultural context. While there is some evidence to suggest that kinship ties weaken when economic resources strengthen (Roosa, Morgan-Lopez, Cree, and Specter 2002), perceptions of family care appear to be in harmony with the culture in which one is raised.

Summary

The field is ripe for further investigations into cultural variations in family routines and rituals and their affects on individual development. It is somewhat surprising that the empirical literature is sparse in this regard. This may be due to several factors. First, there has been a tendency to examine variability across ethnic groups in terms of differences rather than similarities (Allen, Fine, and Demo 2000; Parke 2000). These differences are typically examined across such structural themes as marital status, household composition, and the age at which different roles are assigned. Second, there is a tendency to focus on differences in content of behavior. The literature reviewed here high-lights how there are differences in the content of religious and cultural celebrations but hardly addresses what these celebrations mean to family members. Third, the literature pays little attention to how cultural practices are systematically blended when families from different heritages merge. This will be a topic of increasing importance as not only countries become more diverse in ethnic composition but families become more diverse in cultural lineages.

These limitations point to the need for a more process-oriented examination of routines and rituals across families of different cultural backgrounds. As pointed out by Goodnow (2002), a procedural change is warranted in cultural studies of the family: "Assume, for example, that what provokes one's interest is the presence of some specific difference in practices: in the everyday ways of telling stories, talking to children, keeping them close or letting them run, putting them to sleep, showing them what to do, encouraging their participation in activities or in social groups. Exploration of that kind of difference should be linked to views of culture as a set of practices and to questions about the sources and impact of particular routines" (242). Attention to differences then becomes a search for understanding context rather than a catalogue of variations in practice just for the sake of comparison. If we consider the practice of daily routines and creation of meaning in rituals as the family's response to culture, there are expanded opportunities to enrich theories behind cultural variations.

We have identified a few clues as to how routines and rituals carry out the work of socializing individuals into the mores of the culture. The repetitive nature of daily tasks and conversations held in routine settings such as mealtimes reinforces cultural values for independence or the collective needs of the group. Simultaneously, personal transgressions are framed as part of the cultural dialogue of what is considered good conduct in the context of the family and the larger society. Cultural practices evolve to mark rites of passage that mark developmental transitions for multiple members of the family. Often, these rituals signify a shift in roles in the family to conform to the predominant values of the culture.

Underlying the place of culture in the study of family routines and rituals is the concept of obligation to family. While personal obligation is often framed as part of a discussion that considers familial duty aligned with non-Western societies (Fuligini et al. 2002), in general it is pertinent to the cultural context of family routines and rituals. Within the confines of cultural boundaries, families and individuals make decisions about how to organize their daily lives. A part of this decision-making process, whether conscious or not, is the degree to which individual members actively participate in family gatherings.

Cultural codes of conduct dictate full participation. I have discussed variations in participation at the dinner table in terms of how much time children spent in active conversation with adults. I also noted whether the topic of conversation was geared toward events that happened to the child or the group's future plans. In this regard, participation is regulated in such a way that either accomplishments of the individual are given due recognition or the group's needs predominate. In a similar way, cultural codes regulate who is allowed to participate in the daily chores of the household, such that in some cases extended kin are welcome to walk through the front door unannounced but in other cases need to call ahead. These subtle rules of engagement illustrate the complex nature of cultural regulation of routines and rituals in family life.

To date, knowledge about how individuals understand and ascribe meaning to their sense of obligation to family has been limited. The diary study of Chinese adolescents showed that the sense of obligation to family did not interfere with peer relationships and a balance was struck between time with family and time with peers that did not compromise the adolescents' well-being (Fuligini et al. 2002). These findings shed caution on premature assumptions that just because an individual is living between two cultures there will be a stronger pull towards one than another. Adolescence is a period noted for consolidation of the symbolic and representational aspects of family rituals. Perhaps with greater attention to the symbolic meanings attached to cultural family practices, we can expand our notions of family obligation beyond duty and incorporate the role of belonging and membership in new ways.

5

Family Health

I now turn my attention to family health. In some regards, the link between routines and health makes intuitive sense. The reader can no doubt identify a host of daily routines that are followed, or prescribed, for individual health. Taking vitamins, exercising regularly, and brushing teeth can be seen as routines beneficial to individual well-being. The reader also surely recognizes how difficult it is to maintain some of these routines over time. The best-intentioned New Year's resolutions often fall short of execution because they involve alterations in routines that are difficult to sustain. In many ways, though, these routines can be more accurately described as habits.

Habits are repetitive behaviors that individuals perform often without conscious thought. Behavioral habits are done automatically and typically involve a restricted range of behaviors. For example, chewing on a pencil while deep in thought can be described as a habit. A routine, by contrast, involves a sequence of highly ordered steps (Clark 2000). A morning routine may include a sequence of bathing, having breakfast, reading the newspaper, and having a cup of coffee. Healthy (or unhealthy) habits are often embedded in routines. Being in the habit of eating a nutritionally balanced meal may rely, in part, on shopping and cooking routines.

The distinctions made in this book relate to how families organize activities and how relational commitments are experienced in rituals. Thus, my focus in considering family health is on how family members may support routines associated with health outcomes and how family relationships may protect individuals from stresses associated with different chronic conditions.

Defining Family Health

In considering health variables, the focus is typically on such individual markers as blood pressure, weight gain, or symptoms associated with a chronic condition such as diabetes or asthma. Family health, by contrast, expands the focus to include parameters of interaction and group expectations of healthy functioning. Family health can be considered a group-level phenomenon that includes the "household production of health" (Denham 2003) that affects multiple members as they seek to obtain, sustain, and regain maximum health. A series of in-depth interviews of families living in rural communities has identified categories of health routines associated with dietary practices, sleep and rest patterns, activity, dependent care, avoidance behaviors, medical consultation, and health recovery (Denham 2002). Families organize their activities through a variety of identifiable routines aimed at supporting healthy child development, preventing disease, coping with illness and recovery, and communicating with health professionals. Folded into the rhythms of everyday life, eating, sleeping, and activity routines have the potential to contribute to individual health as well as reduce family-level stresses associated with chronic conditions.

A focus on family health shifts attention from interventions aimed at patient-biologic approaches to a consideration of the social contexts in which disease management takes place. A report of the National Working Group on Family-Based Interventions in Chronic Disease pointed out that disease-management behaviors occur in a relational context and that family members must be included as part of educational and psychosocial interventions (Fisher and Weihs 2000). Family relationships affect chronic disease outcomes in at least two ways. First, the emotional climate of relationships may increase or decrease stress associated with physiological functioning. High levels of conflict and negativity have been found to suppress immune functions and alter physiological responsiveness (Kiecolt-Glaser, McGuire, Robler, and Glaser 2002). Second, family members are involved in management and self-care behaviors that are sometimes "tedious, repetitive, and invasive" (Fisher and Weihs 2000, 562). The repetitive nature of management activities can set the stage for creating routines. Conversely, the repetitive demands may also disrupt routines already in place and threaten family stability. A small but burgeoning empirical literature suggests that routines associated with health behaviors and the affective investment in family rituals may promote better physical functioning.

Health Behavior Routines

Regular family-based routines have been associated with better health for individuals with a variety of chronic conditions. One series of ethnographic interviews identified family routines that promoted better glycemic control in adults with diabetes (Gerstle, Varenne, and Contento 2001). Individuals with better glycemic control made use of nutrition education by including multiple family members in mealtime routines. In one case, daughters adapted their own schedules to be home on time to prevent their mother from eating too late and risking hypoglycemia. One daughter also scheduled her weekly grocery-shopping trip to include her mother so she could shop for fresh fruits and vegetables that were not available at the local delicatessen where she previously shopped. The authors point out that the more family members were involved in predictable management tasks (scheduling doctors' appointments, providing transportation to the pharmacy, meal planning), the better equipped the diabetic was to follow the recommendations of the nutritionist. In contrast, families that refused to adapt their routines according to the demands of the condition (offering sweet desserts at the end of every meal, eating at irregular times, discouraging the importance of daily exercise) not only essentially assured that the patient would not only fail to improve their habits but eventually led to poorer glycemic control than before the educational program. Thus, family members can support or derail recommendations made by health professionals.

Establishing Disease-Management Routines

A series of studies coming out of the Syracuse University Family Research Lab has examined the effects of disease management routines on health and adjustment in children with a chronic illness. In collaboration with physicians at National Jewish Medical Research Center in Denver Colorado and Upstate Medical University in Syracuse, New York, I have been leading a team of researchers who have been collecting medical information and interviewing children and adults about the effects of chronic illness on family life. Most of this effort has been directed at the study of pediatric asthma and adherence to medical regimens. Poor pediatric asthma management has serious consequences, including repeated hospitalizations, emergency care, missed school days, and compromised physical activity. Current practice guidelines emphasize the importance of daily and regular monitoring of asthma symptoms and detailed action plans in the event of an attack (NIH 1997). Many of the recommendations are framed as part of the family's daily or weekly routines, such as vacuuming the house once a week, cleaning duct systems monthly, and monitoring peak flows. Accordingly, asthma management becomes part of ongoing family life and those families who are more capable of the organization of family routines are expected to have more effective management strategies.

We developed a brief questionnaire that asked parents to identify whether there were regular routines associated with filling medications, reminding their child to take medicine, housecleaning, and the amount of burden associated with asthma-management routines. Several questions pertained to medication use, and we identified this as the medication routines factor. The second factor we identified reflected the amount of perceived burden in carrying out these routines. We found in a sample of 153 families drawn from two geographic regions that the report of regular medication routines was related to how well children adhered to their prescribed medication protocol (Fiese, Wamboldt, and Anbar 2005) (fig. 5.1). We looked at three different ways in which medication adherence could be reported: electronic monitoring collected over a period of a year, parent recall of medication use in the past twenty-four hours, and questionnaire responses to how many times the child forgot to take his or her medication in the past week. Based on previous research and clinical experience, we did not expect the children to take their medicine as prescribed all the time. We also expected that parents would tend to report that their children took their medicine more regularly than would be recorded on the computerized monitoring device. Both predictions held true. Regardless of how medicine use was reported, however, we did find that more medication routines in the household resulted in better adherence to prescribed protocols (figure 5.1).

We also found that parents who reported more medication routines had less trouble reminding their child to take his or her medications and that overall their child rarely or never forgot to take their medications. This may also be important from the child's perspective, as a more organized plan may reduce nagging and constant reminders that often lead to conflict, which in turn is associated with poorer medical adherence (Wamboldt, Wamboldt, Gavin, Roesler, and Brugman 1995). To illustrate this point, I offer this description of daily management provided by one family.

> When Frank was two weeks old, he got a virus and was hospitalized for it, and I didn't think he was going to get asthma from this, I really didn't. We could kind of deal with it, but it slowly got worse as time went by. I was kind of up already on things to do as far as taking carpets out of his room, changing curtains, things like that to keep him from coughing, watching for stuff that might be triggering it. The worst part came when he started having seizures from the medication. That was the worst. That was the worst because we weren't sure and even the doctors were a little bit worried, like "What are we going to do?" That was really hard for us, really hard, just really so depressing, and I thought, wow, then I guess the only thing we could do next was to try and eliminate everything that was causing it. So we did—he didn't have any carpet in his room. We wet-mopped the room all the time. We just changed a lot of stuff like that.
>   The whole family is up on it, and they listen more when they hear stuff about asthma. They see brochures and

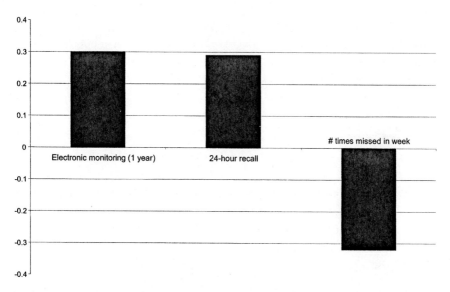

Figure 5.1: Medication routines and medical adherence. Graph represents correlations between different forms of reporting adherence to taking medications and parent report of medication routines.

they're more aware of what asthma does, and you know, like his brother will say something like: "Frank has asthma. We should watch this." Or "Listen to this. They're talking about asthma." I think it has made everybody just a little bit more aware of stuff like that. We get information. We pick up a lot of stuff, like at the pharmacy they have the tapes on how to use your inhalers and stuff like that, and the kids will pick them up. His brothers and sisters will pick things up. We just kind of watch out for him.

In this example, not only are medications filled on a routine basis, but a trip to the pharmacist is an opportunity for multiple members of the family to participate in the health care of the child with asthma. Indeed, these team-based routines and management strategies are associated with better medical adherence and less urgent care (Fiese and Wamboldt 2003).

There are other examples whereby routines are associated with better physical health. Mothers of children enrolled in Head Start who reported more regular routines around eating, sleeping, and playing had children who were considered healthier based on school health records (Keltner, 1992). Likewise, infants raised in households with regular routines have shorter bouts of respiratory infections (Boyce et al. 1977).

The influence of predictable routines on general health is not limited to young children. In a national study of adolescent health, more than twelve thousand students were interviewed about their health behaviors and completed questionnaires about family activities and support (Resnick et al. 1997). Although not designed specifically as a study on family routines, the questionnaire featured several relevant items: number of different activities engaged in with mother and/or father in the past four weeks; parental presence before school, after school, at bedtime, or at dinner; and parent-family connectedness. Cigarette, alcohol, and marijuana use was related to parental presence at routine times such that the greater parental presence, the less likely the adolescent was to smoke cigarettes, abuse alcohol, or smoke marijuana. Although accounting for a small but statistically significant amount of the variance, these findings corroborate studies conducted with younger children and show the potential effects of family routines on behaviors that can lead to better overall health and well-being.

Routine Disruptions under Challenging Health Conditions

Thus far, I have discussed how family organization and structure may affect child health. Children's health status can also affect family functioning, however. In a series of studies examining the effects of caring for a child with cystic fibrosis (CF), disruptions in the marriage and parent emotional distress were identified as potential risks. Caring for a child with CF involves daily medical treatments including regular "chest pounding" to clear the child's lungs. Daily recreational activities are replaced with medical treatments. In a diary study of daily caregiving activities, mothers of children with CF reported greater role strain than mothers in the comparison group of relatively healthy children (Quittner et al. 1998). The researchers found that daily stressors such as bedtime and discipline routines were associated with emotional distress. Given my previous examination of the gendered distribution of household chores, it is also interesting to note that mothers generally reported more role strain and daily stressors than fathers.

Direct observation of mealtime interactions with children with CF supports the proposition that the child's health status can affect daily routines. Families who have a child with CF are additionally challenged to get their children to eat. Extending beyond concerns about "finicky eaters," assuring the health of children with CF includes dietary recommendations of 120 percent to 150 percent Recommended Daily Allowance (RDA) of caloric intake to maintain weight. Mealtimes are often cited as the most frequent household problem by parents of children with CF (Quittner, DiGirolamo, Michel, and Eigen 1992). In observations of mealtimes with preschool-aged children with CF there were noted group differences in comparison to healthy controls. Families who had a child with CF had more difficulty communicating, monitoring affect, and controlling behavior than families without an ill child (Speith et al. 2001). The authors speculate that for families with a child with CF, mealtime routines are simultaneously a normal parenting task and an illness-specific task. Attention to caloric consumption may become the driving force of the interaction and thus bring increased potential for conflict and disruption. Rather than providing respite from hectic activities of the day, mealtime becomes equated with illness management and, perhaps, becomes a burden. Indeed, parents of children with CF and children with feeding problems engage in more directive behavior during mealtimes and feel less effective than parents without children with feeding problems (Sanders, Turner, Wall, Waugh, and Tully, 1997).

Recall that during the early child-raising years regular routines are associated with parental competence and feelings of efficacy. When routines are challenged by problematic behaviors or heightened demands, there is the possibility that parents feel less competent and more frustrated in their regular parenting activities.

Potential Mechanisms of Effect

How to integrate these relatively diverse sets of findings? First, it appears that predictability and order in the household are associated with better overall physical health for children, adolescents, and adults. There are several potential mechanisms to explain these relations, the first of which is the modification of health behavior. In the case of chronic illnesses such as asthma and diabetes, health behaviors include regular administration of medications and daily attention to the prescribed protocol (in the case of diabetes, diet and exercise; in the case of asthma, implementing environmental controls such as housecleaning and avoiding exposure to cigarette smoke). Creating regular routines may facilitate adherence that in turn should result in better overall health and fewer disease symptoms.

A second potential mechanism is that routines promote involvement and monitoring of behavior. For infants and young children, regular routines may be associated with predictable mealtimes that promote better nutritional habits. For example, parents' report of the importance of family routines has been associated with children's milk intake and likelihood of taking vitamins in low-income rural families (Lee, Murry, Brody, and Parker 2002). During the preschool and early school years, if mealtimes are rushed and interactions are marked by discouragements and conflict, children are at greater risk to develop obesity (Drucker, Hammer, Agras, and Bryson 1999; Johnson and Birch 1994). Futhermore, if mealtime routines are regularly accompanied by television viewing rather than conversation, children consume 5 percent more of their calories from pizza, salty snacks, and soda, and 5 percent less of their energy intake from fruits, vegetables, and juices than children from families with little or no television use during mealtimes (Coon, Goldberg, Rogers, and Tucker 2001). In the case of adolescents, parental presence at routine times may be associated with closer monitoring of the adolescents' behavior—a factor known to reduce risky health behaviors. Yet, there is a potential cost if the routines become rigid and are dominated by health concerns, such as in the case of children with CF.

The third mechanism may be through involvement and affective connections. In order to more thoroughly examine this factor, I will consider how family rituals and their emotional component may contribute to family health.

Healthy Adaptation and Emotional Regulation

Thus far I have discussed only the predictability and orderliness of routines in relation to family health. Consistent with the distinctions made in the preceding chapters, I now move to how family rituals and/or the emotional connections made during collective gatherings affect health and well-being. Returning to the study of pediatric asthma and management routines, the discussion now expands to include the emotional strains associated with routine care as well as potential protective factors associated with family rituals. The previously mentioned study regarding medication routines identified a factor labeled Routine Burden (Fiese et al., 2005). The questionnaire items associated with this factor included perceptions that disease management is a chore and that role assignment is somewhat haphazard. We found that responses to these items were associated not with medical adherence but with parent and child quality of life. Parents who reported that asthma care was a chore (and presumably not easily folded into the routines of daily life) also reported that their child's asthma affected their own physical and emotional health (fig. 5.2). Furthermore, children raised in environments with heightened burden reported that they wheezed more, woke more often in the middle of the night, and worried more about their health.

Routines appear to carry an emotional weight for some families. The emotional investment often associated with family rituals is replaced with an emotional drain that can contribute to poorer health. In many cases, parents are overwhelmed and burdened by health care to the extent that they delay treatment and respond to health symptoms only when they become extreme rather than using preventative strategies. The following interview excerpt provides an example.

Well, we more or less suspected that she had asthma for a while. A doctor who wasn't her regular doctor several years ago suggested that she had asthma and had given her a breathing treatment one time when she had a cold or something—I can't remember, but her regular pediatrician, when he saw her, said, "No, she doesn't have asthma,"

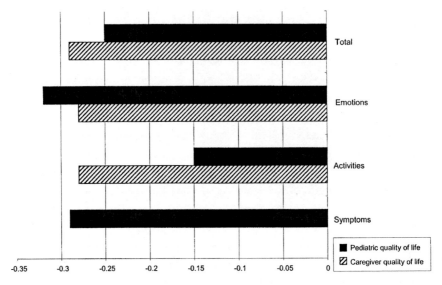

Figure 5.2. Routine burden and quality of life. Graph represents correlations between either caregiver report of their quality of life and routine burden or child quality of life and caregiver report of routine burden. Symptoms refers to how much the child's physical symptoms affect them; activities refers to how much daily activities are disrupted by the disease; and emotions refers to how much the individual worries about the disease symptoms. Lower scores on Quality of Life reflect poorer daily functioning.

so we sort of suspected she might have asthma but we weren't really doing anything about it. And I guess, you know, I noticed more that she complained about feeling tight in her chest or whatever, and she was doing some wheezing. But I come from a family where my mother was a hypochondriac, and I know from my own experience when kids don't want to go to school or something, they make up things about why they don't want to go, so I just choose to ignore a lot of it. Finally then one night she was upset about something—I think we had an argument or something, and she was crying. It was late at night—it was about 10 o'clock at night, and I was very angry with her, and she was complaining about this tightness in her chest and she needed to get to the doctor, and of course I just thought it was a way to get my attention and I was ignoring her, but she kept insisting so, as angry as I was, I loaded her in the car in the middle of the night [and] we went to the emergency room.

These findings are not unique to parent-child relationships but may also extend to other caregiver-patient relationships. In a study of adults with chronic pain (Bush and Pargament 1997), caregivers and patients were asked about pain-specific effects on family life (disrupting family life or making it a burden) and pain-specific adjustment such as dealing with sleep disruption. The researchers reported a different pattern of results depending on whether the patients' or caregivers' responses were considered. For patients with chronic pain, family routines (as measured by the Family Ritual Questionnaire) were associated with the appraisal that family life had been less disrupted by chronic pain. Furthermore, patients who reported more regular family routines also reported less overall pain-specific outcomes. In contrast, the caregivers reported that the meaning associated with family rituals was associated with less disruption and burden in family life. A similar pattern has been noted for children with chronic headaches (Frare, Axia, and Battistella 2002).

The day-to-day management of a chronic health condition involves not only the patient but also the caregiver. For the individual with a chronic condition, knowing when medications are to be taken, who is responsible for communication with health providers, and when meals are to be served may provide a sense of comfort knowing that their needs will be met. For the caregiver, however, garnering meaning from and retaining an emotional investment in family interactions may allow care to be perceived not as a burden but simply as a part of life. Chronic illness can either overwhelm family activities or be made distinct in such a way that the family embraces multiple aspects of family identity (Steinglass 1998). Families who are overtaken and burdened by routine care pay an emotional cost such that family identity is centered on disease-related activities. Thus, individual members come to see their family as an asthmatic family. In this case the disease drives the interactions rather than interactions being measured in response to daily demands. In these instances, the family needs to put the illness in its place such that collective activities can occur outside the realm of disease management. In this regard, the meaning and affect associated with rituals provide relief and at the same time help create a family identity that is multifaceted rather than tied to a single condition.

Family Health Transactions

These two aspects do not operate in isolation and indeed in all likelihood transact with each other over time. Based on the results of the studies reviewed thus far, consider the following scenario. A young child is diagnosed with pediatric asthma. The child's symptoms include wheezing, waking at night, and occasionally restricted physical activity. Responsive parents may note the first sign of wheezing and implement preventative routines (housecleaning, removing animals from the home) and regular administration of medication. The child's symptoms are reduced, and she is able to participate more fully in family activities and gain a sense of identity that is distinct from the chronic illness. Another scenario is also plausible. Caring for the child may be seen as a burden in the absence of predictable routines, and failure to clearly assign roles precludes a clear plan in the case of emergencies. Perceived burden may lead to poorer medical adherence, which results in more symptoms. Faced with a child with multiple symptoms, the poorly managed condition may lead to disruptions in family gatherings by trips to the emergency room. When the rituals are repeatedly disrupted, there is little opportunity to create a positive emotional investment and there is either a dwindling or total absence of rituals. Without the emotional investment and felt security created in these contexts, the child is vulnerable to developing mental-health problems associated with some chronic conditions (fig. 5.3).

Although this pattern is speculative, it does suggest that there are multiple avenues for intervention to put the family back on track. Implementing regular routines may reduce caregiver burden; reducing caregiver burden may result in more positive emotional investment; a more positive emotional investment, in turn, may affect the child's mental health.

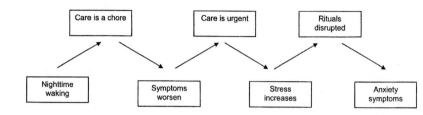

Figure 5.3. Transactional model of disrupted rituals under conditions of chronic illness.

Summary

This consideration of the contribution of routines and rituals to family health highlights how functioning of the individual, at the most basic level, is a group-level phenomenon. Further, the functioning of the group is affected by the health and well-being of the individual. The examination of health routines and chronic-illness management shows that daily care also presents opportunities for burden that can wear and tear on the fabric of family life. Such seemingly minute details as remembering to take medications, eating at regular times, or shopping at a particular grocery store can seem like "just one more thing" that needs attention in an already complicated and stressful situation. Often these responsibilities are assigned to a caretaker who may feel overwhelmed and ill-equipped to restructure the life of the family in response to one family member's health condition. The affected family member, in response, may deny the seriousness of the condition and not want to unduly burden others by shaking up family routines. Serious health conditions cannot be ignored, however, and coping through emergency responding can also develop as one type of routine most often associated with poorer quality of life for both patient and caregiver (Fiese and Wamboldt 2003). Health management is truly a family affair.

My examination of chronic health conditions and management of routine practices also calls into consideration of what happens when a normative task takes on deeper symbolic meaning. For example, in the case of children with CF, receiving enough nutrients throughout the day is a life-or-death matter. Mealtime is not just an opportunity to catch up on the day's events but also one that is carefully regulated for caloric intake. We noted that social interactions were more strained, interactions more controlled, and the routines more rigid than their healthy counterparts. We can thus speculate that when there is a stressor that specifically affects a normative family-level routine such as mealtime, one type of response is to invoke a more rigid structure to the event. I suspect that in the case of families with CF, fear of deviating from dietary guidelines is the predominant concern at mealtime, which places added strains on the gathering. There are other instances, however, where the opposite pattern is observed. Daily routines are not always altered even when an individual's health is compromised. For example, we have witnessed cases where children with respiratory illnesses are exposed to tobacco smoke and other known environmental toxins. In some cases, parents report developing routines believed to reduce the child's exposure such as always smoking outside or sending the child to his or her room when the parent smokes. Although it is doubtful that such tactics are successful in reducing harm, they illustrate how beliefs about connecting behaviors and health may not always be logical. In the case of altering family routines to fit the health conditions of an individual, it is important to first take stock of what routines existed before the diagnosis of the condition and how well-equipped the family is to adjust to new situations. I will return to this point in the chapter on therapeutic interventions.

6

Protective Processes and Family Rituals

A central tenet of developmental psychopathology is that character-istics of the social environment protect children from the negative effects of being raised under high-risk care-giving conditions (Rutter and Sroufe 2000). A key component of this approach is that children are exposed to and engage in a variety of interactions and processes that can promote healthy adjustment even in the face of known risks (Sameroff and Chandler 1975). Indeed, the fact that not all children raised in high-risk conditions suffer psychological harm is the corner-stone of this approach. Much of the current empirical literature I have discussed stems from the groundbreaking work of Wolin, Bennett, and colleagues, who demonstrated the protective function of fam-ily rituals under conditions of parental alcoholism (Wolin, Bennett, Noonan, and Teitlebaum 1980). Promising results from this line of investigation have prompted others to consider the role that rituals may play in protecting children from the harmful effects of divorce, parental psychopathology, and poverty. First I review the seminal work of researchers at George Washington Center for Family Research. Sec-ond, emerging research on the protective role of routines under condi-tions of parental divorce and psychopathology are examined. Third, the potential for routines and rituals to ameliorate some of the harmful effects of poverty are considered.

Preventing Generational Transmission of Alcoholism

The initial work on family rituals and transmission of alcoholism was based in part on the work of David Reiss and his formulation of family paradigms. According to Reiss (Reiss 1981), families create paradigms, or belief systems, that regulate the family's behavior within itself and in relation to the social world. Rituals help preserve these belief systems. A central element in Reiss's proposal is that ceremonial gatherings reflect the family's connections to past generations as well as its extensions outside the family. In terms of family history, repetitive patterns of interaction are rooted in beliefs passed down from one generation to the next. Reiss describes an arm-wrestling ritual of the O'Hara family whereby the sons would routinely arm-wrestle with their father upon his return home. The family legacy was one of achievement and risk-taking: the great-grandfather drilled oil wells at the turn of the century; the grandfather was a farmer and lawyer; the father was a journalist and politician. The arm-wrestling ritual preserved the family's belief that individual success is possible even in the face of adversity.

In contrast to consecrating ceremonials are rituals of degradation. Degradation rituals are not as formally organized as consecrated ceremonials, but they do reinforce roles and reflect the family's beliefs about the trustworthiness of the outside social world. In degradation ceremonies, typically one member of the family is singled out as a scapegoat. Reiss details a pattern of another family in which the youngest son would become interested in something, another child would accuse the boy of damaging or harming something, one of the parents would make an accusation, and other members would ridicule the youngest son. In one instance, the son is accused of harming a hermit crab by putting sand in the bucket. The rest of the family is convinced that sand will harm the crab, and they accuse the youngest son of intentionally hurting the crab and ridicule him for being stupid.

Both of these examples illustrate how repetitive interactions can reinforce feelings of group membership, as in the case of the O'Hara family, or alienate and mock, as in the second case. Not only do these interactions reinforce beliefs within the family, but they also reflect the family's trust with the outside world. In the case of the O'Hara family, the social world is understandable, is manageable, and presents opportunities for success. In the second case, the social world is not to be trusted and only information shared by family members is used to guide behavior. After all, no one questioned whether sand would harm the hermit crab; they only saw that it was an opportunity to degrade the youngest son. These conceptualizations are important in considering the role that rituals may play in protecting children from high-risk care-giving environments. Families who consecrate the past in an affirming and generative manner are more likely to create meaningful and affectively positive rituals. By contrast, families who use their gatherings as an opportunity to deride others and disengage from the social world may place their children at additional risk.

Patterns of Intergenerational Transmission

As pointed out in the first chapter, three types of rituals can be distinguished: family celebrations, family traditions, and family patterned interactions. These rituals may be differently disrupted or maintained under conditions of parental alcoholism.

In interviews of families where at least one parent met the criteria for alcoholism or problematic drinking, three types of families were identified that differed in the degree to which rituals were affected by heavy drinking (Wolin and Bennett 1984). Distinctive families were characterized by the ability to keep family rituals separate from heavy drinking. These families maintained their family celebrations and mealtimes with little noted change when one parent exhibited problematic drinking. Subsumptive families were characterized by a high degree of ritual disruption such that holidays and dinnertimes were subsumed by attention to the alcoholic partner and previously established patterns of interacting were replaced with the more erratic behavior noted in alcoholic families. Between these two groups were families labeled as intermediate subsumptive. These families reported that they were able to maintain their annual celebrations but that dinnertimes were more susceptible to disruption. The likelihood that alcoholism would be transmitted to the younger generation was highest in the subsumptive families.

Young couples have the opportunity to break away from problematic patterns through the creation of a new ritual heritage. In a follow-up study, married children of alcoholic parents and their spouses were interviewed regarding their dinner-time and holiday practices in their family of origin and their contemporary family (Bennett, Wolin, Reiss, and Teitelbaum 1987). Coders who did not know the purpose of the study rated the interviews along six dimensions: (1) level of ritualization in each origin family for dinner and holidays; (2) ritual disruption under impact of parental alcoholism for dinner and holidays in alcoholic families of origin; (3) degree of similarity in family heritage between the couple and each origin family; (4) extent of ongoing contact between the couple and their families of origin; (5) level of deliberateness in family heritage selection; and (6) evidence of novel elements in the family identity of the current generation. Several of these variables were predictive of transmission of problematic drinking. In general, when the child in the couple is a son of an alcoholic father, the couple is at greater risk for becoming alcoholic. Couples who were the most deliberate in planning their own family heritage were the least likely to evidence problematic drinking. Additionally, when the spouse came from a family where dinnertime was highly ritualized, the couple was more protected from transmission of alcoholism. Consistent with the earlier study, couples were less likely to become alcoholic when dinnertime was distinct from problematic drinking.

The protective influence of family rituals may stem from selective engagement and disengagement (Wolin, Bennett, and Jacobs 2003). In the origin family, there is the process of selectively disengaging the alcoholism from daily routines such as mealtime. Second, the child disengages from the family and chooses a spouse that allows for engagement with another family. Third, the couple has the opportunity to disengage from the harmful influences of alcoholism and create their own heritage and customs. In addition to the process of engagement and disengagement is the notion of flexibility and adaptability. Under some circumstances, alcoholism can lead to a rigidity in interaction styles that prevents adaptive change during developmental transitions (Steinglass, Bennett, Wolin, and Reiss 1987). If drinking behavior drives patterns of interaction, there is little tolerance for flex-ibility in responding. In the clinical literature, explosive interactions are sometimes noted when an alcoholic member is confronted or there is an attempt to change the drinking routine. In this regard, rigid ritualization can serve to exacerbate rather than protect children from the potentially harmful effects of parental alcoholism. Rigid interac-tion patterns are probably also more likely to afford opportunities for degradation and ridicule.

In a study of 241 college students and their parents, I exam-ined the potential for the meanings of rituals to protect children from alcoholism and health-related symptoms (Fiese 1993). Adolescents who reported problematic drinking in their family of origin gener-ally reported less meaning associated with their family rituals. There was little difference in parental report. Adolescents raised in alcoholic households who did report significant meaning in their family rituals were less likely to develop problematic drinking themselves or experi-ence anxiety-related health symptoms. Interestingly, parents and ado-lescents in nonalcoholic households were more likely to share similar views of their family rituals than parents and adolescents in alcoholic households. This discrepancy suggests that members of the same fam-ily may often see family gatherings differently when one member is an alcoholic. In these cases, parents may report maintaining their rituals but adolescents may perceive a sense of forced order. In this regard, what is meaningful for the parent may be hollow and perfunctory for the adolescent.

The early work on the potential for rituals to protect children from the harmful effects of parental alcoholism has led other research-ers to consider how organized daily routines and meaningful rituals are disrupted or maintained under other stressful conditions. Divorce is one risk condition that has been studied in this regard.

Maintaining Family Rituals Following Divorce

Divorce has the potential to disrupt family routines and may increase children's risk for developing mental-health and school-related prob-lems. However, not all children exposed to divorce develop problems (Hetherington and Kelly 2002). In a study of 341 children whose parents were divorced, the regularity of bedtime routines predicted academic performance two years after the initial assessment (Guidubaldi, Cleminshaw, Perry, Nastasi, and Lightel 1986). Regularity of bedtime routines was also associated with fewer school absences and better overall health as rated by a school psychologist (Guidubaldi, Perry, and Nastasi 1987). Children and adolescents raised in divorced households also reported fewer internalizing and externalizing symptoms when their custodial parent reported regular assignment of roles and routines in the family (Portes, Howell, Brown, Eichenberger, and Mas 1992).

The effects of divorce on children are not limited to school-age and adolescent offspring. In an interview study of adult children whose parents divorced after the children were eighteen years of age, researchers found that adults were distressed by the loss of family traditions (Pett, Lang, and Gander 1992). Specifically, religious holidays, Thanksgiving, birthdays, vacations, recreational activities, and daily contact such as dinnertime were described as being highly affected. The degree to which the children reported that their parents' divorce disrupted their lives was strongly associated with alterations in family celebrations. These young adults also reported that the divorce presented challenges as they created their own traditions. Many were unsure how to plan for their own family gatherings and whom to include or exclude. Recall, when we considered the developmental life cycle of the family that rules for inclusion and exclusion are often vague in the case of divorce and remarriage.

When parents remarry following a divorce, adolescents often feel displaced and distanced from their family. The regularity of family routines may protect them from distress and feelings of alienation. In a sample of ninety-five adolescents living in remarried households, regularity in household time and routines was associated with adolescents' satisfaction with family life (Henry and Lovelace 1995). The authors speculate that regular routines decrease the amount of time and energy allocated to discussing family management, which in turn may decrease potential opportunities for conflict. It is also plausible that regular routines afford more opportunities for sharing activities with the new spouse, which in turn may influence how the family adapts over the long run to the new partner (Greene, Anderson,

Hetherington, Forgatch, and DeGarmo 2003). Clinicians reinforce the role that traditions and rituals may play in successful adaptation to remarried households. "Successful stepfamilies have worked out positive rituals and appreciate the creativity and cooperation that accompanies these decisions" (Visher, Visher, and Palsey 2003, 169). The early stages of remarriage may be particularly important for establishing a sense of home (Whiteside 2003). The negotiation of daily schedules and alterations in pre-established routines adds to the creation of a new family identity.

In general, the empirical research in this area is somewhat scant. Clinicians have identified different transition periods associated with divorce such as immediately after divorce and the early stages of remarriage. Researchers should be informed by these observations and include time since divorce and reorganization of multiple households in future endeavors. These preliminary findings suggest that the field may be ripe to examine more closely how routines and rituals may protect children from some of the risks associated with parental divorce.

Risks Associated with Parental Psychopathology

Before Bossard and Boll's seminal work, a social worker speculated on how family routines are disrupted in the face of serious mental illness. Mary Bosworth Truedley of Wellesley College published a report in 1946 that drew from medical records of patients who had been hospitalized for serious mental illness (Treudley 1946). Taking a rather revolutionary perspective on the family, she examined family reactions to mental illness rather than considering how family dysfunction may directly cause mental illness. Treudley noted that one characteristic symptom of mental illness is the inability to fit into a normal routine. She observed that disruptions in mealtimes were of particular concern. "Any realistic study of family life discloses how much it is centered around food. In no area does mental illness play a more unfavorable part. Indirectly, it contributes to malnutrition because it usually lowers the family income and thus cuts into the food budget. But its direct undermining of the family health and morale around the dinner table is less generally perceived" (239). More than fifty years ago, Truedley speculated that in the face of a parent's serious mental illness, young children may not be routinely fed, digestion may be affected by an unusual atmosphere at the table, and exposure to intense emotions during "ordinary happenings" can have detrimental effects. Although the empirical literature is not extensive in this area, recent research suggests that some of Truedley's earlier observations may be supported.

Parental depression has been noted as a particularly harmful child-raising condition. Children of depressed parents are at higher risk for developing depression and other mental illnesses (Downey and Coyne 1990). Although the literature is not extensive on the potential for routines and rituals to protect children under this condition, there is some promising preliminary evidence. A group of parents were interviewed about their family-of-origin traditions as well as their current family practices (Dickstein et al. 1999). The researchers identified three groups of families: (1) mother had received a diagnosis of depression and was currently depressed; (2) mother had received a diagnosis of depression and was not currently experiencing depressive symptoms; and (3) mother had no history of psychiatric diagnosis. The family-traditions interview was coded for the degree to which relationships were seen as rewarding and trustworthy. Mothers who were currently experiencing depression cast their family of origin in a more negative way than either the no-illness group or the group not currently experiencing symptoms. Interestingly, husbands of the currently depressed mothers also cast their family of origin in a more negative way. We know that depression tends to run in families and across generations. The results of this study suggest that when depressed parents think about their family of origin, they perceive their traditions as settings where relationships were unrewarding and potentially rejecting. It is not clear whether the current level of depression is clouding perceptions of the family of origin or unresponsive and hostile relationships in the family of origin led to depression.

These researchers have also demonstrated that parental psychopathology influences patterns of interaction during routine mealtimes (Dickstein et al. 1998). Maternal depression was associated with overall family functioning observed during a twenty-minute mealtime observation. In cases where there was maternal psychopathology, it was more difficult to accomplish tasks associated with the meal and affective involvement was less well regulated. In addition, poor general functioning observed during the mealtime was associated with maternal functional impairment. Consistent with previous studies, the cumulative risks associated with maternal psychopathology (that is, level of distress, life stressors, large family size, minority status, maternal education, and low-paying job status) were most strongly associated with impaired family functioning. Although we cannot chart the course of routine disruptions in response to compromised parenting from these cross-sectional studies, we can speculate on some of the inherent processes. It is not unreasonable to expect that when experiencing a serious mental disorder such as depression, it is more difficult to carry out routine tasks such as mealtime. As demonstrated in this study, affect was less well regulated during the course of the meal, as there was erratic attention to how others were feeling. Over time, emotional resources may become drained to the extent that daily routines are haphazard and afford fewer opportunities for positive social interactions. Similar threats exist under conditions of poverty.

Routines and the Challenges of Poverty

In the opening chapters, I examined the role that time plays in organizing and stabilizing routines. Implicit in that discussion was the notion that families have adequate resources to manage time. In some cases, time may be money. When examining the daily rhythms and routines of low-income families it becomes clear how financial resources contribute to time management. An important observation has been made that social timetables are embedded in institutions that operate primarily on public time (9:00 A.M. to 5:00 P.M.) (Burton and Sorensen 1993). However, when there are limited financial resources, daily activities such as traveling to and from work, arranging for childcare, and making medical appointments extend across multiple timetables.

A group of researchers followed seventy-five low-income mothers over four years to study their daily schedules (Roy, Tubbs, and Burton 2004). Information drawn from semi-structured interviews reveals the complex demands on time and scheduling routines in low-income conditions. Approximately half of the mothers were employed full-time, and half of those worked a standard nine-to-five shift. The other half, however, worked during second, third, or "off" shifts. Time spent on public transportation consumed at least two and up to five hours each day. Because of the time consumed by travel to work and poor quality of neighborhood grocery stores, shopping trips were relegated to weekend activities sometimes requiring additional assistance for childcare. Many of these mothers relied on their own mothers to assist in childcare and the grandmothers were frequently responsible for meal preparation. The picture that the researchers paint is one of multiple time demands and a keen attention to coordinating public and private schedules. "For poor mothers with fewer resources, the shifts from picking up children to dinner preparation, from waking, feeding, and grooming children to dropping them off on the way to work, were more than simply hectic. They bore sole responsibility for synchronizing these activities" (173).

Being pressed for time often led to feelings that daily routines were out of the personal control of these hardworking mothers. Relying on others and on public transportation left little flexibility in their daily routines. There were instances of serious consequences to the children. For example, one family had a child with asthma who frequently required unscheduled care at a local clinic. The unpredictability of the child's health condition compromised the mother's ability to maintain a job where there was little tolerance for her missing work to take her child to the doctor.

This line of investigation certainly calls into question the link between adequate resources and family routines. What is striking about these descriptions is that these low-income mothers were not unmotivated or ill-equipped to carry out routines. On the contrary: their days were highly structured and relied on careful coordination of schedules, not unlike those of highly paid CEOs. What is missing from this picture, however, is the ability to translate routines into predictable and assuring patterns of behavior. The authors offer three strategies that mothers used to organize their family time: staggering obligations, expanding resources, and decreasing obligations. What these strategies have in common is organizing time in such a way that regular connections with children were a priority and that by changing the mix of social support, resources, and transportation led to more

predictable and expectable routines. These successful but economically strapped mothers considered predictability of routines essential
to the health and well-being of their children.

These qualitative findings are consistent with other reports documenting the potential for predictable routines to decrease the effects of poverty on children. Predictability at mealtime and bedtime
were identified as correlates of social competence in African-American
children enrolled in Head Start (Keltner 1990). The presence of predictable routines is also associated with academic achievement, school
engagement, and reduced behavior problems in boys raised in urban
and rural low-income families (Brody and Flor 1997; Seaton and Taylor 2003).

The link between financial resources and routine practices is not
well-articulated, nor is it likely simple. There is some evidence that
routines such as mealtime and regular family outings are directly affected by poverty status (Bradley, Corwyn, McAdoo, and Coll 2001).
Whereas the interview data (Roy et al. 2004) highlights the intersec-
tions among managing time, routines, and financial resources, the
quantitative data (Brody and Flor 1997; Seaton and Taylor 2003) suggests that the effects of routines on child outcomes are mediated by
maternal self-esteem and optimism. Consistent with the literature
linking family routines and parental competence, parents often have
to make hard choices to manage their daily lives when faced with
limited economic resources. If they are able to create an organized
environment for their children through such measures as enforcing
homework time and regular mealtimes, the parents feel more competent, which in turn affects the child's competence. There may be some
circumstances, however, where the link is more direct. Brody and Flor
(1997) report that for African-American boys there was a direct link
between family routines and academic achievement and internalizing
problems. The researchers speculate that the boys in this sample were
at heightened risk for poor outcomes such that the routines played a
more proximal role in protecting them from risk.

It would appear that in order to carry out a routine it is necessary to have a minimum amount of resources available. If the bulk of
a parent's energy is spent negotiating transportation schedules and arranging for childcare, there may be little time or energy left to monitor

homework or bedtime routines. By contrast, if the parent is optimistic and thinks that the family has adequate resources to carry out routines, then a sense of self-efficacy becomes associated with the daily practice and may indirectly affect children through more positive parenting and engagement.

Protective Processes and Routines and Rituals

Under high-risk child-raising conditions there appear to be at least four processes to consider when evaluating the potential for routines and rituals to serve a protective function. First, there is a strong generational component to risk as well as to protection. Many high-risk conditions are embedded in a long history of distress that extends across generations. Breaking the cycles of alcoholism, depression, and poverty may rely, in part, on altering belief systems. If the family holds a shared belief that relationships are manageable and the social world outside the family can be trusted, then a firm foundation may be laid to create meaningful rituals. Again there is the dilemma of whether beliefs lead to routines or the repetitive practice of routines leads to strongly held beliefs. Because rituals often extend across generations, it is likely that elements of beliefs and practices are both transmitted. When maladaptive patterns are being carried across generations, the family must identify which elements are harmful and which elements may be preserved. This leads to the second aspect of protective processes.

The cycle can only be broken when families are aware enough of their practices that they can deliberately plan new behavior patterns. Rather than succumb to lethal legacies, individuals must take the initiative to plan and carry out new practices that cement positive interactions across time. In this regard, parenting in high-risk conditions requires conscious attention to activities that under less stressful conditions often happen effortlessly. Whereas we have discussed how the repetitive nature of routines is often unconscious, when resources are limited either financially or emotionally, conscious decisions need to be made in planning daily life. This focused effort can, under some circumstances, lead to additional strains that prevent the smooth implementation of routines, which in turn may affect feelings of competence and efficacy. If, on the other hand, resources can be allocated to maintain regular routines there is the possibility that stress is reduced and efficacy increased.

Third, along with deliberate planning, clear boundaries and the distinctiveness of routines need to be preserved. To protect multiple members of the family from high-risk conditions, it is sometimes necessary to disengage from problematic exchanges as well as keep routines distinct from the associated risk condition. This was most clearly demonstrated in the work on alcoholism and family rituals. However, the same principle can apply to other risk conditions. For example, adolescents raised by parents with depression fare better if their parents are able to identify when they are in a depressive state (Focht-Birkerts and Beardslee 2000). In this regard, the illness is made distinct from daily patterns and reduces the likelihood that the child will feel responsible for either chaotic or unresponsive interactions.

Fourth, adequate social support and resources need to be in place to carry out predictable routines. These resources extend to social institutions such as schools, healthcare clinics, and child-care facilities. For parents facing multiple economic and emotional challenges, the world outside family life often works against maintaining a cohesive household. Juggling transportation, childcare, and medical needs can tax parents to the point of having little energy left for organizing routines. Even when parents are well-intentioned, extensive demands outside the home may prevent physical presence within the home. Society can ill afford maintaining public institutions that work against families maintaining stability and predictability in their daily lives.

Summary

We began this chapter relying on one of the basic tenets of developmental psychopathology: that characteristics of the environment can serve to protect some children from the negative effects of high-risk child-raising conditions. A basic tenet of developmental psychology is that there is a "self-righting tendency" under some risk conditions. That is, under many conditions there is a tendency for an organism to "right itself" once it has been disturbed. For example, premature infants born at low birth-weight tend to "catch up" to normal weight by two years of age given adequate nutrition and care. Routines offer one way for families to get back on track or "right themselves" when there is exposure to risk. The clearest case of this is reorganization of the family following divorce and remarriage. There may be other cases where families respond to limited resources by focusing on organizing timetables in a way that provides structure and predictability in what can be considered an otherwise chaotic lifestyle. This response to stress, however, is strikingly different than our consideration of family's response to chronic illness in the previous chapter. As noted there, in some cases families responded through increased rigidity in their routines in an attempt to reduce concerns and fears about their child's health conditions. In the case of limited economic resources we note conditions of inflexibility associated with burden. The solution for these economically strapped mothers was to gain control of their routines by reducing obligations and increasing flexibility. Thus, notions of rigidity and flexibility must always be taken into context.

We also learn that rituals are used to engage and disengage from the family. As a group, the family can choose to disengage from the social world, creating its own unique myths often at the emotional cost of an individual member. An individual family member may also disengage from the rituals of the group as a way to preserve his or her emotional integrity. This can be seen as a healthy disengagement when family rituals are primarily regulated to maintain problematic and destructive behaviors. It is also likely that under these troubling circumstances the healthier individual creates beliefs about family rituals that are distinct from the rest of the group. These non-shared views may allow for an easier exit from the fold as well as pave the way for a redefinition of family roles, the theme of the next chapter.

7

Therapeutic Forms of Routines and Rituals

Is it possible to use rituals as a means for effecting change? Thus far, I have highlighted how each family creates unique patterns of behavior that come to have meaning and contribute to a family identity. In this chapter I discuss how family routines and rituals may be orchestrated to change behavior. Primarily, there are three ways that rituals have been used therapeutically. First, rituals are prescribed and conducted as part of family therapy. Second, therapists have used routines as a way to change disruptive behavior in home and school settings. Third, home-visiting programs have used the family's daily routines as a setting to implement prevention programs.

Rituals in Family Therapy
Milan Group

There is a long history of using rituals in family therapy, and the very nature of psychotherapy has ritualistic elements. Appointments are made at the same time every week, typically there is a ritualized beginning and ending to the session, and considerable attention is paid to symbols and affect. The roots of using rituals in family therapy can be traced back to the Milan group led by Mara Selvini-Palazzoli

(Selvini-Palazzoli, Boscolo, Cecchin, and Pratta 1977). These therapists emphasized the prescription of rituals to address such issues as
bereavement, eating disorders, and aggressive behaviors. These initial
efforts relied heavily on the family implementing prescriptions drawn
up by the therapist, not unlike making a trip to the pharmacist to treat
an infection.

Several of these cases are highly noted in the literature. One of
the first to appear was a description of a family whose son died in the
hospital after suffering brain damage during birth. The family's two-
and-half-year-old daughter became anorectic and was not told about
her brother's birth or death. The therapist instructed the parents to
tell the daughter about her brother and prescribed a funeral in which
his baby clothes were buried in the garden. In this case, for whatever
reason, the family was unable to deal directly with their loss. Carrying
on daily routines as if nothing was wrong surely sent mixed messages
to the young girl. By making their grief public via the funeral, the
parents helped their daughter make sense of what had happened and
gave themselves an opportunity to grieve more openly.

Although Selvini-Palazzoli does not directly address why the
daughter was not initially told of her brother's death, the case calls to
mind Reiss's model of family paradigms. The family created a closed
belief system that prevented them from making use of information
that, albeit painful, was necessary to incorporate into their rituals.
The cutting off of emotion is one of the central characteristics often
noted by family therapists in cases that may benefit from a ritual intervention. Based on the assumption that rituals evoke strong affect,
ritual interventions in these situations can release powerful feelings.
The ritual itself provides a holding place for these emotions that eventually may allow the family to recognize and adjust to the suffering
they experienced in the past.

The Milan group also developed a form of ritual intervention
called the "even-odd day" approach. In one reported case, the family
rigidly holds the belief that all members of their extended clan are
upright individuals. One of the daughters has been wrongly treated
by one of the cousins but cannot say anything because of the belief system enforced by the family. The daughter refuses to eat and
develops anorexia nervosa. The therapists prescribe an even-odd day

intervention whereby on alternate days the entire family is to gather in the dining room and lock the door for one hour. One by one, each family member is allowed to vent his or her feelings (including those associated with the extended family) uninterrupted for fifteen minutes. By engaging the group in a common activity, feelings can be expressed more directly and the daughter can be supported in ways that decrease her need to exert control by not eating. Alternating days changes the rules that families use to enforce myths and brings problematic behaviors into greater relief.

The Milan group emphasized the prescribed nature of rituals and rarely attended to their symbolic nature, but rituals clearly have symbolic components, as in the funeral for the baby boy. Onno van der Hart extended the work of the Milan group to include the symbolic and at times nonverbal aspects of ritual interventions. For van der Hart, "Rituals are prescribed symbolic acts that must be performed in a certain way and in a certain order, and may or may not be accompanied by verbal formulas"(van der Hart, Witztum, and de Voogt 1988, 62). The blending of ritual prescription with attention to the symbolic meaning of family beliefs is central to contemporary family therapy. Evan Imber-Black, Janine Roberts, and Richard Whiting have edited the most extensive source material on rituals in family therapy. Rather than detail the entire volume, I will highlight some of the key points made by these talented therapists.

Ritual Themes in Therapy

Five themes have been identified that therapists can use in implementing ritual interventions: (1) membership; (2) healing; (3) identity; (4) belief expression and negotiation; and (5) celebration (Imber-Black 2003). The reader will recognize that these themes are similar to those we have examined in regards to the family life cycle. Many of the rituals that therapists have designed can help assist families make the transition from one part of the life cycle to the next. They note many idiosyncratic family situations that do not allow for a smooth transition through widely accepted practices. For example, rituals associated with divorce, adoption, homosexual marriage, and handicapped member's leaving home must be designed anew. In some instances the rituals are not created because they call into play the public nature of the transition, as in some homosexual unions. In other cases, although there may be societal acceptance of the family structure, there are few customary rituals to note the transition. For example, remarriage involves adding new members to the family and negotiating which rituals will be maintained and which ones will be discarded.

Remarriage involves not only creating new rituals but also managing multiple households, attention to legal matters, and inclusion of children in the decision-making process. The creation of new family traditions can ease the strains associated with remarriage (Whiteside 2003). Part of the transition period in remarriage is negotiating who is expected to attend which events. At the most mundane level are expectations for attending meals. When children split time between two households, it is important to identify a time when the households can be together. One way to define membership is through residence at any time during the month. If a child spends weekends at one household and weekdays at another household, then a weekend or a special day of the month can be set aside for stepbrothers and stepsisters to be together. These gatherings may initially be forced and met with resistance but may take on new meaning over time. This transition can only be made, however, if there is clear communication about expectations for attendance and constructive conflict resolution.

Remarried families often note vacation time as a challenging and potentially rewarding time to create new traditions. Whiteside (2003) provides examples where vacations sometimes present a comedy of errors and creative solutions. One family reported that the father in one household had "custody" of the tent and failed to include the center poles when he lent the tent to his former wife. Although the situation was an opportunity for derision and conflict, it was used as a time to joke with the new stepfather and became the subject of a new family story. Creative solutions such as drawing straws for the sofa bed, renting a van to accommodate everyone, and grouping children by age rather than genetic heritage provide opportunities to create new family traditions that extend across multiple households.

Rituals in family therapy can also aid the healing process following loss. In some regards, contemporary culture often works against the healing process after death. Most people die at a hospital far removed from family members, eulogies are offered by individuals who barely knew the deceased person, and children are often "protected" from the sadness and grief expressed during a funeral. In a case described by Imber-Black (2003), a young woman presented herself for therapy because she could not "finish anything." She had dropped out of college, was living alone after two failed relationships, and had trouble finishing her work. Her mother had died when she was fourteen, and upon recommendation from the family physician she did not attend the funeral because it would be "too upsetting." Soon after her mother's death, her father sold the family home and they moved to another community. She was unable to attend her junior high school graduation and began to experience problems finishing her work in high school. Given her bereaved state, her teachers accommodated her. She expressed the wish to return to her family home, where she felt closest to her mother. Her father refused, saying it would be too painful for him. Fourteen years later, she still expressed a desire to return to her family home. The therapy was directed toward expressing her loss and preparing to return to her family home for a visit. The home was a setting for many ritual practices, and the return home symbolized a connection to the past and helped her recognize that places, as well as people, change. Once she was able to make the pilgrimage she was able to put to rest her feelings of unfinished business and return to her college studies. The therapist comments that the success of this case was allowing the daughter to identify the returning home ritual rather than suggesting a visit to her mother's gravesite, which held little meaning. In this healing ritual, the daughter was able to connect with the past and move on to a new future.

The systematic proscription of celebrations can also be used therapeutically. Holiday time can present many challenges to families who have experienced either a loss or significant transition. Often it is what is not said or done that is reflective of the family's functioning. One family had created a holiday tradition of making a holy wreath to encircle a photograph of the father who had died several years before. Upon remarriage, no one took the initiative to bring out the photograph or make the wreath at Christmas time. The youngest daughter became quite distraught because she had seen this as a comforting connection to her deceased father. The therapist was able to persuade the daughter to talk about her feelings of loss during the holidays and re-implement the ritual of placing the wreath on her father's photograph (Whiteside 2003).

The use of rituals in family therapy rests on similar assumptions about the power of ritual described in this book. Rituals are highly symbolic and carry with them emotions that can be forcefully charged. Disruptions of rituals due to illness, remarriage, or loss can threaten family functioning because behavioral guideposts have been taken away. "How do I act at the dinner table where the foods have changed and my stepfather insists we sing grace?" "Can we still go to the farm and cut down our Christmas tree when Dad has to be in a wheelchair?" A recurrent theme in the clinical literature is how quickly rituals can disappear without comment. Indeed, much of the therapeutic literature is aimed at identifying rituals and making public what individual members hold private. In some regards, the goal of clear and direct communication is no different than other forms of therapy. However, in this instance the enactment of a previously treasured practice can reinforce emotional bonds in the context of open communication. This pairing of emotion, deliberate action, and direct expression gives power to ritual interventions. Just as anthropologists have described the power of ritual to connect past, present, and future, therapeutic interventions of this sort afford the opportunity to recognize past legacies, interpret their significance in the present, and look to the future for hope and change.

Thus far, I have discussed the therapeutic use of rituals as part of the psychotherapy process. This approach rests on several basic principles of psychotherapy such as formation of a therapeutic alliance, conducting part of the therapy in a consultation space separate from the family's home, and attention to the effects of past relationships on current functioning. A second way that family routines have been used as a form of intervention is behaviorally based and often implemented at the family's home.

Home-Based Routine Interventions

Not surprisingly, families who seek assistance with their child's problematic behaviors often recount disruptive behaviors during the course of regular routines. Getting ready for school, weekly trips to the grocery store, bedtime, and mealtime are often settings where parents will report the occurrence of difficult behavior. Indeed, most parents will recognize that even infants will have what is provincially called "poison time." Take a stroll through a grocery store between 3:00 P.M. and 5:00 P.M. and no doubt there will be several very unhappy children and many irritable parents. In these cases, tiredness and hunger may contribute to the experience of stepping into a hornet's nest during a routine trip to the grocery store. In most cases, the children can be soothed after a nap or a meal. In other cases, however, demanding exchanges persist and problematic behaviors disrupt regular family routines.

Perhaps the most notable interventions are implemented at either mealtime or bedtime. Approximately 25 percent of children display some form of sleep disturbance (Mindell 1993). The persistence of sleep disturbances can lead to increased fatigue in parents, which in turn can lead to less patience for lengthy bedtime routines. One form of intervention recommended by pediatricians to deal with a child's sleep disturbance is the implementation of "positive bedtime routines." The intervention is aimed at teaching appropriate pre-bedtime behavior and sleep-onset skills. This approach is based on the notion that young children may use pre-bedtime activities to prolong engagement with other family members, which ultimately leads to a later sleep-onset time and increases the likelihood of bedtime tantrums. This approach first suggests moving bedtime to a later time in the evening to coincide more closely with the child's natural sleep-onset time (Milan, Mitchell, Berger, and Pierson 1981). Parents are then instructed to engage in a series of relaxing activities with their child before bedtime. A key aspect of this portion of the intervention is following each activity with praise and signaling transition to the next activity. In this respect, there is the opportunity for the pre-bedtime routines to turn into rituals because of the emotional connections paired with the activities. Once the activities are well established and the child is able to fall asleep quickly, the child's bedtime is systematically moved earlier to coincide with the original bedtime goal. Bedtime routines have been found to prevent long bouts of crying, result in fewer tantrums, and reduce parental frustration (Kuhn and Weidinger 2000).

In a creative approach to treating bedtime problems, a bedtime-story intervention was implemented with four children between the ages of two and seven (Burke, Kuhn, and Peterson 2004). Parents reported that all of the children resisted going to bed three or more nights a week for more than four weeks. The intervention consisted of setting clear bedtime expectations and implementing a contingent reward system for staying in bed (for example, placing a small prize or charm under their pillow before they awoke the next morning). Parents read a bedtime story titled *The Sleep Fairy* to the children (Peterson and Peterson 2003). The tale describes two children who have difficulty going to sleep but are visited by the Sleep Fairy if they stay in bed. The Sleep Fairy places a small gift under the children's pillow if they stay in bed throughout the night. Sleep onset improved for all children during the intervention. Total sleep time improved at three-month follow up for half of the children. This small study gives promising evidence to suggest that implementing a new routine may help regularize sleep patterns.

Mealtime interventions have been implemented in situations where the child exhibits unruly and disruptive behavior. These interventions fall under the larger umbrella of parent management training (PMT). PMT employs strategies to facilitate parents' disciplinary skills to help manage child misbehavior. Interestingly, PMT programs include several elements of structural family therapy where there is an emphasis on reinforcing hierarchy and roles (Minuchin 1974). This approach rests on the assumption that healthy family functioning depends on clear boundaries between parents and children and that it is parents' right and responsibility to guide their children's behavior in a socially acceptable manner. An often-overlooked element of PMT is the balance of positive support and encouragement with clear and decisive disciplinary tactics. Some evidence suggests that the effectiveness of PMT is calibrated by the ratio of positive to negative behavior. The exact ratio may range from four-to-one to seven-to-one (Cavell 2001). This balance is relevant to the discussion of the affective and emotional bonds created during routine events as well as the proscription of socially acceptable behavior.

When routine events such as mealtime are disrupted, the opportunities for positive emotional exchanges are significantly decreased.

Most meals last, on average, twenty minutes. If over half of this time is spent in struggles and disciplinary actions, there is little time left to experience and process the positive aspects of the day and meal. If we take the conservative estimate of a four-to-one ratio of positive to negative emotional experiences, then adaptive mealtime exchanges should include sixteen minutes of supportive and responsive exchanges, balanced by four minutes of discipline and attention to behavior control. This is, of course, speculative but may be a practical guidepost for families and therapists.

Behavioral interventions conducted in such routine settings as bedtime and mealtime are aimed at reducing problematic behavior and teaching children how to act in socially acceptable ways. We do not know whether these interventions are more effective when implemented during the course of a regular routine or if they encourage changes in behavior patterns across the day. We do know that implementing behavioral interventions in the context of daily routines clearly marks when parents should employ techniques learned from the therapist and helps the therapist identify the settings of problematic behaviors (Lucyshyn, Kayser, Irvin, and Blumberg 2002). In this regard, routine interventions may be simpler to implement because they make it easier for parents to remember when to use their new skills. Future program development may help us better understand whether there is something unique about implementing a routine intervention and its ability to foster long-term behavioral change. This leads us to the third form of routine intervention, home visitor programs.

Home Visitor Programs

Home visitor programs have a long history of attending to family organization and structure. Home visitors include nurses, family-life educators, and social workers. Often, home visits are made as part of prevention programs aimed at reducing harm in high-risk child-raising conditions. Several notable programs have been developed for teenage mothers, low-income families, and parents of children with physical handicaps. I will highlight some of the general principles of home visitor programs that attend to routines and rituals and then provide examples from specific programs.

Guides exist for home visitors in creating sleep, feeding and eating, and toileting routines in families with young children (Klass 2003). One of the main tasks for home visitors is to educate parents about normative development and place their child's behavior into an expectable pattern. For example, a home visitor may talk with a parent about naptime. The first objective is to educate the parent that most babies between four and eight months of age need a morning and afternoon nap. The next step is to assist the parent in developing activities such as rocking, cuddling, or singing soft lullabies to ease the child into the nap routine. Even with infants, routines are used as transitions from one point to another.

Feeding and eating routines provide an opportunity to educate parents about nutrition and the importance of developing autonomy and independence. The home visitor's role is to encourage children to feed themselves at an appropriate developmental stage so that children learn that mealtime is a social occasion for the family. Recognizing that newfound independence can result in throwing food off the table, refusing to eat, and developing finicky tastes, the home visitor can educate parents about substituting foods, limiting snacks, and creating a casual eating atmosphere to reduce the likelihood of struggles. Klaas writes: "If parents themselves enjoy cooking and eating and provide a relaxed mealtime, their young children will probably adopt this attitude toward eating. Mealtime then can be a special family time of shared enjoyment—a time which children know their parents are eager to chat with them and with each other" (Klass 2003, 273).

Toilet training can present challenges for even the most educated and experienced parent. Home visitors are likely to hear from parents that they feel pressured to toilet-train their children at an early age. Whether directly stated or implied, imperatives from grandparents and nursery school administrators often create undue anxiety and worry for parents. Home visitors can assist by helping parents recognize when their child is ready for toilet training. Developing toilet-training routines also involves creating a new language. Children and parents must come to some agreement about how to name different body parts and functions. Even the activity itself can take on a new vocabulary—"going to the potty," "visiting the little boy's room." No doubt, many of these phrases have family roots that may go back generations. Initiating the routine itself demands a balance between parental support and child autonomy. In this situation, the home visitor can provide guidelines as to how to take a relaxed attitude toward training and not to expect overnight miracles. This routine calls for patience on the part of the parent as the child becomes more and more in control.

Large-scale prevention programs that employ visiting home nurses have documented reductions in child abuse and increases in parental sensitivity (Olds 2002). These programs have been effective in part by increasing parental self-efficacy. Although not explicitly stated in published reports, many of the activities fostered by the nurses revolve around routine play and feeding.

Thus far, I have examined the potential for routines and rituals to assist therapists and educators in altering patterns of behavior. Because family therapists, parent trainers, and home visitors may employ different techniques, each treatment must be fine-tuned to meet the needs of an individual circumstance and particular family style. In the concluding section of this chapter, I examine how an assessment of the family's existing routines may lead to more systematic and tailored interventions.

The Four R's of Routine Interventions

Most clinicians will agree that a "one size fits all" approach to effecting family-level change rarely works. Although there are several empirically validated forms of child and family therapy (Kazdin 2003), deciding which form of intervention will best fit the unique needs and circumstances of a particular family is still a challenge. A model proposed by Sameroff and colleagues suggests that an examination of the relative strengths and weaknesses of an existing family system leads to at least three possible forms of intervention: remediation, reeducation, and redefinition (Sameroff 1987; Sameroff and Fiese 2000). To this triad, I add a fourth form of intervention applicable to an assessment of family routines: realignment (Fiese and Wamboldt 2001).

The "Four R's" of intervention are rooted in the transactional model that suggests behavioral change is not the result of changing characteristics of an individual but is part of developmental regulatory systems and reciprocal interactions between parent and child (Sameroff 1995; Sameroff and Chandler 1975). For the purposes of this discussion, there are several key elements of this model. First, any single behavior is seen as part of a larger system that operates under identifiable regulatory principles. At the most basic level, families are regulated to maintain balance, or homeostasis. This is one of the reasons it is so difficult to effect change at the family level. Second, there is the potential for behavior of one individual to affect and change the behavior of another individual. Although it is common to expect that parents can affect the behavior of their children, it is also reasonable to expect that children affect the behavior of their parents in a transactional manner. Third, cultural and family codes regulate these patterns of interaction such that the expression of any behavior is embedded in cultural and family values. My colleagues and I raised all these points as we considered how routines and rituals affect development and are affected by such conditions as chronic illness, culture, and poverty.

On the surface, a routine such as going to bed may appear to be linked only to an individual, but how it is carried out is dependent on the organization of the family as a whole. Each member has the potential to contribute to the routine and effect change. As noted, developmental changes in the child often provoke changes in family routines and rituals (Fiese et al. 1993). A routine intervention must make sense to the family to be implemented, and it is probably most effective when folded into the everyday rhythms of family life. Now I will discuss each form of intervention as applied to routines and rituals by using the example of managing a childhood chronic illness, pediatric asthma.

Remediation

Remediation is most frequently targeted at changing the child's behavior in a way that ultimately changes the behavior of other members of the family. Once the child's behavior is changed, the family has little need for further interventions and is able to stabilize in a relatively short period of time. For children with moderately persistent to severe asthma, a daily regimen of medication use is prescribed. The most typical scenario is the use of medication twice a day, once in the morning and once in the evening. Interestingly, national guidelines suggest that children use their medication after they brush their teeth in the morning and evening (NIH 1997). This assumes, of course, that the child regularly brushes his or her teeth twice a day. If this is indeed the case, then the tooth-brushing routine can be paired with medication use. The child and parent are instructed to put the medication next to the toothbrush as a reminder. If the child is able to follow this routine, then it decreases the likelihood of a struggle over taking medication and attention to adhering to the regimen is limited to this one setting. In some cases, routines have been disrupted to the extent that they need to be redefined for healthy family functioning.

Redefinition

Redefinition of routines occurs when pre-existing routines or rituals have been disrupted in such a way that the child's behavior is not well regulated. As noted in the chapter on family health, diagnosis of a chronic illness has the potential to disrupt family routines to the extent that previously adaptive interactions are overtaken by the illness. In these cases, it is important for the family to redefine the routine in such a way that it preserves family emotional bonds. In the instance of pediatric asthma, bedtime reading routines may have been replaced by medication routines. In these instances, the parent's worry and concern about the child taking his or her medication occupies the space previously dedicated to the comfort of a bedtime story. The bedtime routine needs to be redefined such that it is not subsumed by attention to the illness and the medication routine is made distinct from the affective involvement evident when reading a bedtime story. In these instances, the parent's worry and concern needs to be addressed and redefined such that a previously established ritual maintains its meaning. In some cases, routines may exist but they have been disrupted by conflict. These instances call for realignment.

Realignment

Family members sometimes do not agree upon the importance of particular routines. In these instances, conflict and disagreement prevents the smooth implementation of a routine. Somewhat surprisingly, I have found that parents (and grandparents) may disagree on the importance of taking daily medications for children with asthma. These disagreements may be rooted in past experiences ("I had asthma as a kid and never needed any medication") or misinformation about the effects of particular medications ("He will get hooked on drugs so he shouldn't take it"). A skilled clinician will be able to evaluate the root of these beliefs and help dispel myths. At the family level, it is important to address the conflict in such a way that the parents can agree on the importance of a particular routine. The effectiveness of this resolution rests on several features: (1) the willingness of the disagreeing parties to cooperate; (2) the degree to which each member values routines; and (3) the ability to separate marital conflict from managing daily routines. Not surprisingly, families going through divorce often experience such disagreements. In these cases it is important to clarify to the parents the importance of a particular routine for the health and well-being of their child. It is also important to work with the parents to implement the routine in such a way that there is minimal "spill-over" from marital tensions. When the child is faced with living in two households, it may be particularly important to come to an agreement about some consistency in routines (for example, bedtime, mealtime, medication use) so that the child is protected from the harmful effects of conflicting households.

Reeducation

The fourth form of intervention is termed reeducation. This type of intervention is directed toward parents who lack the requisite skills or information to carry out routines. Although this might appear to be a relatively straightforward form of intervention, in some regards it may be the hardest to implement and maintain. Parents who have had little experience with regular routines in their families of origin may have few behavioral markers to guide them in creating new routines. It is important to first consider what experience parents have had with regular routines. If the parent comes from a family where there was considerable rigidity, routines may have been associated with abusive relationships. If the parent comes from a family where there was considerable chaos, it will be important to find a common language to talk about the importance of routines. Returning to pediatric asthma as an example, basic education in the importance of daily medication use as well as routine preventative measures (duct cleaning, minimizing exposure to tobacco smoke, avoiding allergens) should be the starting point. The next step is to examine the family's tolerance for implementing new routines. Because implementing routines raises the possibility of more close contact within the family, it is important to evaluate the potential for the routine to be emotionally provocative as well as soothing. In this regard, it may be easier initially to educate families about basic routines that are relatively well contained and time limited before developing routines that have the potential to turn into affectively charged rituals. Thus, implementing a bedtime routine may be a good start before calling everyone to the table for regular family mealtimes.

Clinical Decision-Making

These four forms of intervention can be applied to systematic clinical decision-making (fig. 7.1). First, the clinician should evaluate whether routines are present. This can be done through semistructured interviews in which the family is asked to recount a typical day from morning to evening with targeted questions about the behaviors of interest ("How do you handle the child's medication?"; "What happens if he or she forgets to take their medication?"; "Do you have a backup plan?"). If routines are present and have not been disrupted by the current stressor, remediation is a likely intervention. If routines were present in the past but have been disrupted due to the stressor, redefinition is in order. But if the family is not currently practicing routines, two evaluations need to be made. Is there conflict in the family that is getting in the way of carrying out routines? Has the family had any previous history of carrying out routines? If the answer to the first question is yes, then realignment is indicated. If there is little to no conflict but there is no previous family history of routine practices, then reeducation is indicated.

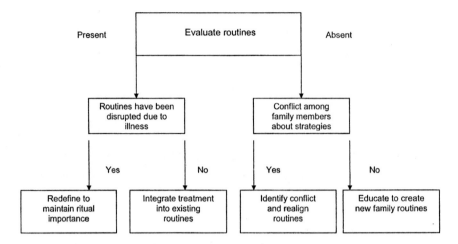

Figure 7.1. Clinical decision-making.

Reflections on Routine and Ritual Interventions

In this chapter I have examined a variety of ways in which routines and rituals may be used to effect behavioral change. Clearly, the work rooted in family therapy was specifically designed using principles of ritual theory. Home-based behavioral interventions and home visitor prevention programs have attended to theoretical aspects of rituals to a lesser extent. It may be important to reconsider the central role of affect and emotion in creating routines and rituals. A recent experience in the Family Research Laboratory at Syracuse University brings home this point. As part of our regular study protocol, we videotape families during the course of a regular mealtime in their home. Research assistants instruct the family in the use of the camera but are not present during the meal. Although there may be an initial discomfort to having the camera present during the gathering, most families settle into their regular routine with minimal comments about the camera or unusual situation. Indeed, most families report that these recorded mealtimes are "typical" or "very typical" of their regular mealtimes. However, in some cases we have observed that the family is unaccustomed to being together. One case in particular stands out.

The family consists of the mother and her only son. There are three television sets on although there are only two members of the family. As the mother puts the food on the table, the son asks to say grace. The mother says that she "can't be bothered" but he can do whatever he wants. For the first five minutes of the meal, the son repeatedly tries to engage the mother in conversation about his day. She fails to respond and instead pays attention to the soap opera on television. As he persists in getting her attention, she becomes very angry and berates the child at the table. At one point the mother tosses a knife into the sink, barely missing the child. Obviously, this is an extremely difficult scene to watch. The child is working hard at family time and trying to engage in what he believes to be a potentially meaningful dialogue. The mother, by contrast, wants nothing to do with the setting or, in some respects, her son. By her own report, she and her son rarely, if ever, eat together. Most often one eats in front of one television in the kitchen and the other sits in front of another television in the living room. In this case, the communal meal seems to have heightened the potential for emotional tension. This family uses physical distance to reduce interpersonal involvement. Calling them to gather together created the opportunity for personal derision rather than affirmation. In this respect, ritual interventions have the potential to call forth strong emotions, some of which can be degrading. This example is offered to highlight that daily routines always have the potential to be affectively charged. Attention to family tolerance and experience with close emotional bonds should be evaluated before implementing a routine intervention that can also have ritual significance.

Summary

When considering therapeutic forms of ritual interventions, I started with the defining characteristics of symbolism and affect. This is not an accident. The therapeutic power of rituals resides in bringing into the open what has been put aside or buried for unspoken and painful reasons. The symbolic nature of rituals allows the family to connect deeply felt emotions to a place, time, or physical object. The ritual stands in place for an unfinished process that then allows the family to make the transition to the next phase of their lives. Therapeutic rituals are also warranted when the symbolic life of the family has begun to slip away, as in instances of loss or remarriage. These are often the hardest to identify because it is the absence of a ritual that is mourned.

Subtle distinctions between routine disruptions and ritual derailments also come into relief when considering therapeutic interventions. Many of the behavioral interventions are aimed at stabilizing family life and reducing momentary disruptions. Although difficulties at bedtime, tantrums at mealtimes, and food refusals are not minimal concerns from a parent's perspective, the interventions are typically circumscribed to a particular routine. If attended to soon enough, routines are likely disrupted for a brief time and once corrected family life goes on with minimal alterations. However, when the family experiences considerable conflict about the importance of either family routines or family obligations, the rituals can become derailed and the costs to family life are more substantial. When rituals disintegrate to the point that the affective life of the family is either hollow or degrading, processes of redefinition or disengagement may come into play. Although some would like to have a cookbook of rituals to provide to clients to ease distress, experienced clinicians will agree that the force of such interventions comes from an appreciation of the journey made between the family's history and the point at which they enter the therapist's office.

8

Promising Prospects

At the outset of this book, I challenged commonly held myths and misconceptions about the relevance of routines and rituals to contemporary family life. Survey and descriptive studies suggest that the practices associated with family routines and affective investment in family rituals hold promising prospects for generations to come. Yet, the explicit ways in which routines and rituals may garner influence have not been addressed. In this concluding chapter, I speculate on some potential mechanisms of effect as well as outlining substantial threats to maintaining routines and rituals.

Mechanisms of Effect: Enforcing a Family Code

The majority of research included in this book is correlational in nature; there are no carefully controlled experiments, extensive longitudinal data, or randomized clinical trials on which to base an evaluation of potential mechanisms of effect. This current state of affairs, however, should not be viewed apologetically. The careful observations made by highly talented researchers have drawn a clear picture of the complexities of family life and showed that some of these processes cannot be distilled into one or two questionnaires nor fully assessed in a single study. As most family researchers will attest, it is both a blessing and a curse to consider the intricate intercorrelations of family-process variables because directions of effects are next to impossible to determine. Rather than become discouraged by these limitations, it may be more fruitful to recognize the transactional nature of family processes and consider what potential mechanisms may be explored in future research.

One way to approach this somewhat daunting task is to consider how families create codes that regulate behavior and emotion. Sameroff has proposed that development is regulated by a series of transactions embedded in an "environtype" much as biological development is regulated by the genotype (Sameroff 1995; Sameroff and Fiese 1992, 2000). Current advances in developmental psychopathology suggest that the demarcation between biology and environment may be an artificial one to the extent that biology is always embedded in a social context and social interactions are affected by individual differences in biology (Cicchetti and Walker 2001). What is relevant to our discussion is how the family creates a code that regulates individual and group behavior. The family code is composed of beliefs and group practices aimed at regulating the behavior of individuals as well as creating a group identity. The family code does not operate in isolation but is influenced by cultural codes as well as individual dispositions. This book has shown examples throughout where societal as well as individual characteristics can contribute to either comforting or taxing family interactions. Looking forward to holiday gatherings practiced as part of religious observances supports cultural codes and can reaffirm the family's beliefs and values. Trying to feed a temperamentally difficult infant and establish regular wake and sleep cycles are more taxing transactions between the family and individual code. The practice of family routines and beliefs associated with rituals provides a context in which the family codes behavior to be aligned with cultural regulations and individual strivings.

I have paid considerable attention to how families can organize their daily lives to support individual development. Setting regular bedtimes, organizing weekly grocery trips, and filling medications on time are examples of how the family regulates individual health and well-being. In addition to the directly observable and reportable practices of families are the shared beliefs held by individual members. Several examples have shown that holding shared beliefs about routines and rituals is related to the individual's satisfaction with family life and/or individual functioning. Beliefs are typically seen as residing within the individual. Representations of relationships are often considered part of the individual's internalized working models of the social world (Bretherton, Ridgeway, and Cassidy 1990). In the case of rituals, when individuals share similar beliefs about the importance and concomitant affective investment of such practices, the representations become part of the family code. For example, I reviewed research that found when couples shared similar views on the importance of religious celebrations, they were happier in their marriages (Fiese and Tomcho 2001) . When adolescents and parents shared similar views about the importance of family rituals, the adolescents were healthier overall (Fiese 1992). When family members hold disparate views, it is more difficult to carry out routines, and thus the opportunities to create affectively positive representations are compromised. In this regard, the working models of family representations are very much grounded in repeated group interactions as well as expectations that others will share somewhat similar views.

Routine Rhythms

Within this dynamic of repeated interactions and creation of shared beliefs, mechanisms of effect begin to become clear. Routine practices appear to establish rhythms and provide guidance for monitoring behavior. At the most basic level, routines may regulate biological rhythms in a transactional manner. Some literature suggests that infants raised in more predictable households establish more regular sleeping and waking patterns (Sprunger et al. 1985). Although it is beyond the scope of the literature to consider exactly how circadian rhythms become part of daily routines, the regulation of individual behavior clearly occurs within the context of the family's daily rhythms. At some point, the individual's regulatory systems must be aligned with the cadence of the group.

Routines are also embedded in cultural rhythms. When low-income mothers have to straddle two or more time domains (public

[9 A.M. to 5 P.M.] and family [5 A.M. to 9 P.M.]), it is more difficult to maintain regular family routines (Roy et al. 2004). Organizing time must conform not only to the proclivities of the family but also to cultural clocks. The daily activities of the family are bounded by what is expected as good conduct and constitute communities of practice within a given culture (Goodnow 1997). Time of awakening, balance between home and work, and entry into school are all examples of how the family clock intersects with cultural timetables.

Behavior Monitoring

A second potential mechanism of effect is how family routine practices support behavior monitoring and family management strategies. Parents keep a close eye on when children are supposed to be home, what homework needs to be done, who is working late, and what plans need to be made for the following day, week, or month. Extensive literature documents the role that behavior monitoring can have in reducing adolescent risky behaviors and preventing academic failure in high-risk neighborhoods (Furstenberg et al. 1999). One time this monitoring takes place is during the course of family routines. It may not be enough that parents know where their children are at any given point in time; they must also regularly engage them in conversations about what happened during the day and anticipated events. Participating in regular routines may promote more monitoring, which in turn provides more opportunities for family engagement. Monitoring is typically seen as something that is imposed on the child rather than as a part of a family process. Routine practices may not only promote monitoring but also reduce resentment of a careful watch because they signify to the individual member that others are involved and care about his or her whereabouts.

Behavior monitoring is regulated in part by cultural constraints. Curfews not only are set by families but also are enforced by the local authorities. In some instances, the family's monitoring practices will be more restrictive than those set by a particular society. However, cultural expectations for when an individual is considered a mature member of society may affect how closely families keep track of the whereabouts of adolescents. For example, I noted that the celebration of a Mexican daughter's fifteenth birthday signifies passage into adulthood as well as a more restrictive watch of the daughter's engagements. The centrality of behavior monitoring may extend across cultures and has been found to reduce the risk of developing depressive symptoms and problematic behaviors for Caucasian, African-American, and Mexican youth (Ge, Best, Conger, and Simons 1996; Gorman-Smith, Tolan, Henry, and Florsheim 2000; Kim and Ge 2000).

The need for and effectiveness of behavior monitoring can also be influenced by characteristics of the individual. My discussion of studies of family mealtimes noted that characteristics of the child influence how smooth or difficult interactions can be. In the case of children with cystic fibrosis, for example, mealtime interactions were more strained and controlling because of concern about the caloric intake of the child (Quittner et al. 1992). In this regard, the individual's characteristics contribute to the overall level of behavior monitoring required.

Establishing daily rhythms and monitoring behavior are essential to the family code of routine practices. The intersection of family routines with individual and cultural features can be depicted schematically. Following the general systems framework outlined by Bronfenbrenner (Bronfenbrenner 1979; Bronfenbrenner and Evans 2000) family routines can be shown as intermediary to the rhythms of the individual and timetables of the culture (fig. 8.1). This is not a static picture, since family routines are adjusted to fit the changing nature of the individual as well as to provide a conduit for the individual's participation as a member of a culture. Whereas family routine practices may effect change through establishing rhythms and monitoring behavior, family rituals may garner influence on a more symbolic level.

Emotional Investment in Rituals

At least two mechanisms appear to contribute to the power of family rituals. First and foremost is the emotional investment in carrying out and participating in rituals. Throughout this book I have noted how affect and symbolic significance are part and parcel of rituals. Family therapists alert us that the cutting off of an emotional experience often warrants a therapeutic ritual intervention. Family rituals provide a

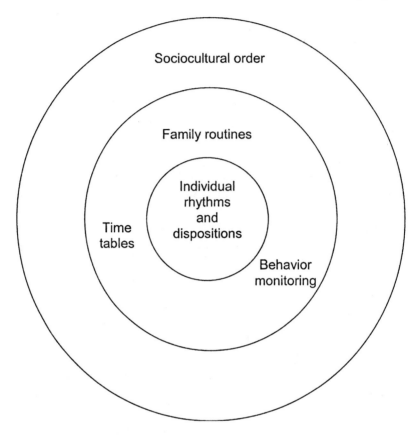

Figure 8.1. Ecologies of family routines.

place where strong emotions can be contained as well as an opportunity to share affectively charged experiences. The very nature of setting
aside time punctuates the emotions associated with a group gathering.
When a routine turns into a ritual, there is often eager anticipation
and occasion to replay past experiences through storytelling or even
in flashbulb memories of a specific event. This emotional connection
provides the foundation for family identity and feelings of belonging
to a group. Under supportive conditions, the individual is a valued
member of the family as well as society. Under less supportive conditions, rituals are sometimes used as opportunities to exclude or deride
others. In both instances, emotions become cemented in the center of
the repeated interactions.

Relational Efficacy

A second potential mechanism of family rituals is self-efficacy. I have noted several instances where predictable routines and meaningful rituals were associated with feelings of personal competence and self-efficacy. In the context of family rituals, this is a relational efficacy rather than a skill set of specific competencies. Feelings of being competent as a parent, worthy of love, or valued as a spouse are all created through relationships. These internalized representations reinforce beliefs that relationships are manageable sources of reward that can be relied upon in times of stress as well as times of celebration. In many regards, this notion is not new. Working models of attachment relationships are created to support individual autonomy and feelings of security between caregiver and child (Bretherton and Munholland 1999). In the case of family rituals, the working models are created to support poignant feelings of individual effectiveness in relating with others as well as belongingness to a group. Although felt security in the group is important, beliefs that relationships can be understood and are manageable incorporate the organizational features of rituals (Reiss 1989). Extending beyond attachment themes is the notion that when gathered as a group there is a need to be able to predict behavior of multiple individuals that includes a sense of order as well as belonging. Much like a fine symphony, the synthesis of individual players, not the individuals themselves, produces the overall effect.

Cultural values support the meaning behind many family rituals. The practice of religious celebrations occurs alongside cultural proscriptions. Rites of passage, replete with symbolism, are one example of the links between family celebrations and societal mores. The shared beliefs created in sociocultural contexts allow for ease of communication and comfort with new situations (Goodnow 1997). As with family routine practices, family rituals can also be represented as a holding place between individual affect and proprieties of culture (fig. 8.2). Although these models are quite expansive and not subject to direct confirmation or disconfirmation, they can provide a useful heuristic in considering how routines and rituals are part of the family code.

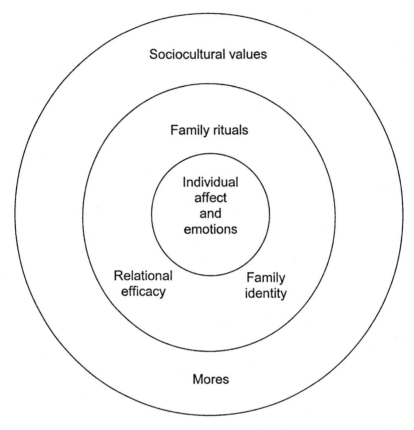

Figure 8.2. Ecologies of family rituals.

Threats to Maintaining Routines and Rituals

I have tried to present an optimistic tone to the study of family routines and rituals, noting their protective influences and potential links to health and well-being. However, there are several societal changes that point to substantial threats to families' efforts to establish predictable routines and meaningful rituals. Historians and family scholars have proposed that family rituals evolved to create private spaces for the family as a retreat from the work world and to protect the needs of the younger generation. The creation of parlor games, spending Saturday evening huddled around the radio, or leisurely Sunday meals were cited as examples of how families demark time and space for collective gatherings. Current trends suggest that for some families, personal space is allocated to create individual sanctuaries rather than communal refuges. A recent survey conducted by the Kaiser Family Foundation of more than one thousand parents of children between birth and six years of age found that 36 percent of those surveyed reported their children had television sets in their bedrooms, and that for families with children between the ages of four and six, the rate was 43 percent (Rideout, Vandewater, and Wartella 2003). Not surprisingly, in households where there was heavy television viewing, adults were less likely to read to their children. These findings suggest that for some families, personal space is being allocated to support screen viewing (both television and computer) that may take the place of face-to-face interactions. In this regard, television viewing and computer use may be a habit that turns into a routine built around personal isolation rather than a family routine based on repetitive patterned face-to-face interactions.

A second threat to family routines is lack of time. Many families are challenged to find time for multiple members to be home at the same time. Shifting work schedules, holding down more than one job, and extensive commitments to extracurricular activities can work against spending time together as a family. A very real concern is how much time is needed to maintain family cohesiveness and predictability. There is no easy answer to this question. The absolute amount of time may not be as important as the perception that some quality time is being spent together. Not surprisingly, family time is valued most when it is spontaneous (Daly 2001). It is difficult to be spontaneous when there is a sense of being tied to rigid schedules. This conundrum is made even more poignant when we consider the availability of economic resources. The findings are somewhat mixed as to whether adequacy of economic resources is directly linked to the practice of regular routines. However, there is enough evidence to suggest that when economic resources are scarce, more measured attention needs to be paid to creating routines, which in turn can compromise spontaneity and positive engagement.

A third threat to the practice of routines and rituals is the use of rituals to exclude family members in a systematic way. I highlighted how weddings can be times of exclusion for gay and lesbian family members. There are other instances where families will selectively choose who to include and who to exclude, perhaps in an attempt to avoid conflict. I recently came across a case study of twenty-one members of a family extending across four generations that describes the evolution of exclusion in one family (Richlin-Klonsky and Bengston 1996). When a member of the oldest generation became ill, she and her spouse were excluded from holiday gatherings because of her poor health. After the woman passed away, her husband was invited to the family gatherings once again. He refused the invitation, remarking that because he and his wife had been excluded for seven years he had no intention of returning to the family fold. When a pattern of systematic exclusion is set into place, membership of the group is restricted in such a way that family identity is characterized by a distrust of the social world that can, in turn, affect the individual's working model of family relationships. There are, of course, times where exclusion can help promote healthier exchanges, but it often comes at a cost to some family members. As our society becomes composed of greater numbers of older adults, many of whom will reach stages of poor health, families will be faced with more situations where they must decide how to include others when there are transitions in living and health conditions. Although exclusion may sometimes be more comfortable, there may be hidden costs to the family as a whole.

A fourth threat is more subtle in nature. With shifting family structures, it is possible for previously established routines to disappear without comment. I noted these effects when examining the role that routines and rituals may play in stepfamilies. When rituals become part of an unspoken heritage, younger generations lose an opportunity to connect with their legacies. The neglect of rituals can also foster feelings of alienation. When confronted with multiple stressors, families often alter their daily routines in order to attend to pressures at hand. We noted that when adapting to care for a child with a chronic illness, families have a tendency to focus on illness-related routines at the cost of previously established family routines. When the routines and rituals slip away, there is an erosion of family fiber that holds the group together. Often, such erosion is not noted until there is a crisis in the family that calls for careful reflection.

Promising Prospects

Although the threats are real, there are also clear opportunities to create routines and rituals that meet the demands of contemporary society. If we can learn from the past, then we can take heart in the fact that rituals evolved historically as a way to protect the family as a cohesive group. Let us take one family routine that can be preserved and may have powerful effects. Throughout the book I have discussed family mealtimes as representative of both routine and ritualized aspects. It is unreasonable to expect that families will spend seven nights a week gathered for an elaborate meal. However, if a family meal is defined as lasting twenty minutes, four family meals require less than an hour and a half each week. Given the results of the surveys and research reviewed in this book, one can expect about ten minutes of the meal to include instances of positive exchange, two minutes of attention to manners, five minutes dedicated to family management issues, and three minutes of up and down time (serving, clearing, and so on). Within this densely packed time frame is the opportunity for daily conversations that can support vocabulary development, active problem solving, and allocation of shared household chores. Thus, there is actually the opportunity to reduce stress and burden by spending twenty minutes in a family meal. The gathering is also an opportunity to share family stories and reinforce relationships that extend across generations.

On the face of it, this may appear to be a naive proposal. However, there is much to be gained from family routines and rituals, and considerable costs if they are absent. It is incumbent upon policymakers to attend to the real challenges and opportunities inherent in organizing family life. Rather than taking a disheartened view that families are overwhelmed and do not have the wherewithal to put order into their potentially chaotic lives, a more optimistic and informed stance is warranted. Policies at the workplace, in schools, and in local and national governments should be developed to foster more rather than less family time. In the workplace, this may mean more flexible work hours and easier access to child care. In schools, this may mean not assigning homework one night a week to create more family time. At the level of local and national government, it may mean educational initiatives to highlight the importance of family routines

and home-based programs to help families create routines when they
have had little previous experience. These initiatives need not be part
of any particular agenda except to show that family strengths are valuable and each family has the opportunity to create routines and rituals
that are meaningful to them.

Returning to Bossard and Boll's seminal work, I close with a
quotation taken from a young adult in their study: "Rituals are what
make family life something firm and substantial; something that will
give you a solid foundation for your later life. In my family, it is the
little things, each by itself unimportant, but put together they spell
family life" (59).

Reading a bedtime story, weekly pizza night, or calling out the
same greeting when returning home are the moments that come to
define what it means to belong to a family. These routine times are
rarely elaborate events nor are they even cause for comment. Yet, they
form the memories and scrapbooks of family life. Just as no two family trees will look alike, the most important rituals for a family will be
the ones that evolved spontaneously and often with a sense of humor.
There are few other gatherings where the simple beginning to a joke
or well-told story can result in a synchronized response by several individuals. The punch line is never the point. Rather it is the sense of
collective belonging and expectation that those around you will not
only understand your idiosyncrasies but celebrate your uniqueness.
Rituals not only connect us to the past but are also the foundation for
a family's future. It is the ordinary routines of family life that make this
important group so extraordinary.

References

Allen, K. R., Fine, M. A., and Demo, D. H. (2000). An overview of family diversity: Controversies, questions and values. In D. H. Demo, K. R. Allen and M. A. Fine (Eds.), *Handbook of family diversity.* (pp. 1–14). New York: Oxford University Press.

Aukrust, V. G., and Snow, C. E. (1998). Narrative and explanation during mealtime conversations in Norway and the U.S. *Language in Society, 27,* 221–246.

Beals, D. E., and Snow, C. E. (1994). Thunder is when the angels are upstairs bowling: Narratives and explanations at the dinner table. *Journal of Narrative and Life History, 4,* 331–352.

Bennett, L. A., Wolin, S. J., Reiss, D., and Teitelbaum, M. A. (1987). Couples at risk for transmission of alcoholism: Protective influences. *Family Process, 26,* 111–129.

Blair, S. L., and Lichter, D. T. (1991). Measuring the division of household labor: Gender segregation of housework among American couples. *Journal of Family Issues, 12,* 91–113.

Blum-Kulka, S. (1997). Dinner talk: Cultural patterns of socialization in family discourse. Mahwah, N.J.: Lawrence Erlbaum.

Bornstein, M. H., Tal, J., and Tamis-LeMonda, C. S. (1991). Parenting in cross-cultural perspective: The United States, France, and Japan. In M. H. Bornstein (Ed.), *Cultural approaches to parenting.* (pp. 69–90). Hillsdale, N.J.: Lawrence Erlbaum.

Boss, P. (1999). *Ambiguous loss.* Cambridge, Mass.: Harvard University Press.

Bossard, J. H. S., and Boll, E. S. (1950). *Ritual in family living.* Philadelphia: University of Pennsylvania Press.

Bowen, M. (1978). *Family therapy in clinical practice.* New York: Jason Aronson.

Bowlby, J. (1967). *Attachment and loss: Vol 1. Attachment.* New York: Basic Books.

Boyce, W. T., Jensen, E. W., Cassel, J. C., Collier, A. M., Smith, A. H., and Ramey, C. T. (1977). Influence of life events and family routines on childhood respiratory tract illness. *Pediatrics, 60,* 609–615.

Boyce, W. T., Jensen, E. W., James, S. A., and Peacock, J. L. (1983). The Family Routines Inventory: Theoretical origins. *Social Science and Medicine, 17,* 193–200.

Bradley, R. H., Corwyn, R. F., McAdoo, H. P., and Coll, C. G. (2001). The home environments of children in the United States, Part I: Variations by age, ethnicity, and poverty status. *Child Development, 72,* 1844–1867.

Bretherton, I., and Munholland, K. A. (1999). Internal working models in attachment relationships: A construct revisited. In J. Cassidy and P. Shaver (Eds.), *Handbook of attachment.* (pp. 89–111). New York: Guilford.

Bretherton, I., Ridgeway, D., and Cassidy, J. (1990). Assessing internal working models of the attachment relationship: An attachment story completion task for 3-year-olds. In M. T. Greenberg, D. Cicchetti, and E. M. Cummings (Eds.), *Attachment in the preschool years: Theory, research and intervention.* (pp. 273–308). Chicago: University of Chicago Press.

Britto, P. R., Fuligini, A. S., and Brooks-Gunn, J. (2002). Reading, rhymes, and routines: American parents and their young children. In N. Halfon (Ed.), *Childrearing in America: Challenges facing parents with young children.* (pp. 117–145). New York: Cambridge University Press.

Brody, G. H., and Flor, D. L. (1997). Maternal psychological functioning, family processes, and child adjustment in rural, single-parent, African American families. *Developmental Psychology, 33,* 1000–1011.

Bronfenbrenner, U. (1979). *The ecology of human development.* Cambridge, Mass.: Harvard University Press.

Bronfenbrenner, U., and Evans, G. W. (2000). Developmental science in the 21st century: Emerging questions, theoretical models, research designs, and empirical findings. *Social Development, 9,* 115–125.

Bruess, C. J. S., and Pearson, J. C. (1997). Interpersonal rituals in marriage and adult friendship. *Communication Monographs, 64,* 25–46.

Burke, R. V., Kuhn, B. R., and Peterson, J. L. (2004). Brief report: A "storybook" ending to children's bedtime problems: The use of a rewarding social story to reduce bedtime resistance and frequent night waking. *Journal of Pediatric Psychology, 29,* 389–396.

Burton, L. M., and Sorensen, S. (1993). Temporal dimensions of intergenerational caregiving in African-American multigeneration families. In S. H. Zarit, L. I. Pearlin, and K. W. Schaie (Eds.), *Caregiving systems: Informal and formal helpers.* (pp. 47–66). Hillsdale, N.J.: Lawrence Erlbaum.

Bus, A. G., van IJzendoorn, M. H., and Pellegrini, A. D. (1995). Joint book reading makes for success in learning to read: A meta-analysis on intergenerational transmission of literacy. *Review of Educational Research, 65,* 1–21.

Bush, E. G., and Pargament, K. I. (1997). Family coping with chronic pain. *Families, Systems, and Health, 15,* 147–160.

Caplow, T. (1982). Christmas gifts and kin networks. *American Sociological Review, 47,* 383–392.

Caplow, T., Bahr, H. M., Chandwick, B. A., Hill, R., and Williamson, M. H. (1982). *Middletown families: Fifty years of change and continuity.* Minneapolis: University of Minnesota Press.

Carlson, E. A., Sroufe, L. A., and Egeland, B. (2004). The construction of experience: A longitudinal study of representation and behavior. *Child Development, 75,* 66–83.

Cauce, A. M., and Domenech-Rodriquez, M. (2002). Latino families: Myths and realities. In J. Contreras, K. Kerns, and A. Neal-Barnett (Eds.), *Latino children and families in the United States: Current research and future directions.* (pp. 1–25). Westport, Conn.: Praeger.

Cavell, T. A. (2001). Updating our approach to parent training I: The case against targeting noncompliance. *Clinical Psychology: Science and Practice, 8,* 299–318.

Cheal, D. (1988a). *The gift economy.* London: Routledge.

Cheal, D. (1988b). The ritualization of family ties. *American Behavioral Scientist, 31,* 632–643.

Cicchetti, D., and Walker, E. F. (2001). Editorial: Stress and development: Biological and psychological consequences. *Development and Psychopathology, 13,* 413–418.

Clark, F. A. (2000). The concept of habit and routine: A preliminary theoretical synthesis. *Occupational Therapy Journal of Research, 20,* 123S–137S.

Clarke-Stewart, K. A., Gruber, C. P., and Fitzgerald, L. M. (1994). *Children at home and in day care.* Hillsdale, N.J.: Lawrence Erlbaum.

Cohler, B. J. (1991). The life story and the study of resilience in response to adversity. *Journal of Narrative and Life History, 1,* 169–200.

Coltrane, S. (2000). Research on household labor: Modeling and measuring the social embeddedness of routine family work. *Journal of Marriage and the Family, 62,* 1208–1233.

Compan, E., Moreno, J., Ruiz, M. T., and Pascual, E. (2002). Doing things together: Adolescent health and family rituals. *Journal of Epidemiology and Community Health, 56,* 89–94.

Contreras, J. (2004). Parenting behaviors among mainland Puerto Rican adolescent mothers: The role of grandmother and partner involvement. *Journal of Research on Adolescence, 14,* 341–368.

Coon, K. A., Goldberg, J., Rogers, B. L., and Tucker, K. L. (2001). Relationships between use of television during meals and children's food consumption patterns. *Pediatrics, 107,* E7.

Coontz, S. (2000). Historical perspectives on family studies. *Journal of Marriage and the Family, 62,* 283–297.

Cowan, C. P., and Cowan, P. A. (2000). *When partners become parents.* Mawhah, N.J.: Lawrence Erlbaum.

Cowan, P. A., and Cowan, C. P. (2003). Normative family transitions, normal family processes, and healthy child development. In F. Walsh (Ed.), *Normal Family Processes* (3rd ed., pp. 424–459). New York: Guilford.

Cowan, P. A., Cowan, C. P., Heming, G., and Miller, N. B. (1991). Becoming a family: Marriage, parenting, and child development. In P. A. Cowan and M. Hetherington (Eds.), *Family transitions.* (pp. 79–109). Hillsdale, N.J.: Lawrence Erlbaum.

Cox, M. (2003). *The book of new family traditions: How to create great rituals for holidays and everyday.* Philadelphia: Running Press.

Crouter, A. C., Head, M. R., Bumpus, M. F., and McHale, S. M. (2001). Household chores: Under what conditions do mothers lean on daughters? In A. J. Fuligini (Ed.), *Family obligation and assistance during adolescence: Contextual variations and developmental implications.* (pp. 23–41). San Francisco: New Directions for Child and Adolescent Development.

Crouter, A. C., Head, M. R., McHale, S. M., and Tucker, C. J. (2004). Family time and the psychosocial adjustment of adolescent siblings and their parents. *Journal of Marriage and Family, 66,* 147–162.

Csikszentmihalyi, M., and Rochberg-Halton, E. (1981). *The meaning of things: Domestic symbols and the self.* Cambridge: Cambridge University Press.

Cummings, E. M., Davies, P. T., and Campbell, S. B. (2000). *Developmental psychopathology and family process.* New York: Guilford.

Curtis, G. (1997, January 19). Leave Ozzie and Harriet alone. *New York Times Magazine,* 40–41.

Daly, K. J. (2001). Deconstructing family time: From ideology to lived experience. *Journal of Marriage and Family, 63,* 283–294.

Davis, J. (2003). Mazel Tov: The Bar Mitzvah as a multigenerational ritual of change and continuity. In E. Imber-Black, J. Roberts, and R. A. Whiting (Eds.), *Rituals in families and family therapy* (2nd ed., pp. 182–214). New York: W. W. Norton.

DeBaryshe, B. D. (1995). Maternal belief systems: Linchpin in the home reading process. *Journal of Applied Developmental Psychology, 16,* 1–20.

Denham, S. A. (2002). Family routines: A structural perspective for viewing family health. *Advances in Nursing Science, 24,* 60–74.

Denham, S. A. (2003). *Family health: A framework for nursing.* Philadelphia: F. A. Davis.

Dettwyler, K. A. (1987). Breastfeeding and weaning in Mali: Cultural context and hard data. *Social Science and Medicine, 24,* 633–644.

Dickstein, S., Seifer, R., Hayden, L. C., Schiller, M., Sameroff, A. J., Keitner, G. I., Miller, I. W., Rasmussen, S., Matzko, M., and Magee, K. D. (1998). Levels of family assessment: II. Impact of maternal psychopathology on family functioning. *Journal of Family Psychology, 12,* 23–40.

Dickstein, S., Seifer, R., St. Andre, M., and Schiller, M. (2001). Marital attachment interview: Adult attachment assessment of marriage. *Journal of Social and Personal Relationships, 18,* 651–672.

Dickstein, S., St. Andre, M., Sameroff, A. J., Seifer, R., and Schiller, M. (1999). Maternal depression, family functioning, and child outcomes: A narrative assessment. In B. H. Fiese, A. J. Sameroff, H. D. Grotevant, F. S. Wamboldt, S. Dickstein, and D. L. Fravel (Eds.), *The stories that families tell: Narrative coherence, narrative interaction, and relationship beliefs.*

Monographs of the Society for Research in Child Development (Vol. 64 [2], Serial no. 257, pp. 84–104). Malden, Mass.: Blackwell.

Douglas, W. (2003). *Television families: Is something wrong in suburbia?* Mahwah, N.J.: Lawrence Erlbaum.

Douglas, W., and Olson, B. M. (1995). Beyond family structure: The family in domestic comedy. *Journal of Broadcasting and Electronic Media, 39,* 236–261.

Downey, G., and Coyne, J. C. (1990). Children of depressed parents. *Psychological Bulletin, 108,* 50–76.

Dreikurs, R. (1948). *The challenge of parenthood.* Oxford: Duell, Sloan, and Pearce.

Dreikurs, R., Gould, S., and Corsini, R. J. (1974). Family council: The Dreikurs technique for putting an end to war between parents and children (and between children and children). Oxford: Henry Regnery.

Dreyer, C. A., and Dreyer, A. S. (1973). Family dinner time as a unique behavior habitat. *Family Process, 12,* 291–301.

Drucker, R. R., Hammer, L. D., Agras, W. S., and Bryson, S. (1999). Can mothers influence their child's eating behavior? *Developmental and Behavioral Pediatrics, 20,* 88–92.

Dubas, J. S., and Gerris, J. R. M. (2002). Longitudinal changes in the time parents spend in activities with their adolescent children as a function of child age, pubertal status, and gender. *Journal of Family Psychology, 16,* 415–427.

Eakers, D., and Walters, L. H. (2002). Adolescent satisfaction in family rituals and psychosocial development: A developmental systems theory perspective. *Journal of Family Psychology, 16,* 406–414.

Eisenberg, M. E., Olson, R. E., Neumark-Sztainer, D., Story, M., and Bearinger, L. H. (2004). Correlations between family meals and psychosocial well-being among adolescents. *Archives of Pediatric and Adolescent Medicine, 158,* 792–796.

Fagan, A. (2003). Poll shows teens value ties, time with family. Retrieved September 23, 2004, from www.washingtontimes.com/national/20030805-113337-717r.htm.

Falicov, C. J. (2001). The cultural meanings of money. *American Behavioral Scientist, 45,* 313–328.

Falicov, C. J. (2003). Immigrant family processes. In F. Walsh (Ed.), *Normal family processes* (3rd ed., pp. 280–300). New York: Guilford.

Fiering, C., and Lewis, M. (1987). The ecology of some middle class families at dinner. *International Journal of Behavioral Development, 10,* 377–390.

Fiese, B. H. (1992). Dimensions of family rituals across two generations: Relation to adolescent identity. *Family Process, 31,* 151–162.

Fiese, B. H. (1993). Family rituals in alcoholic and nonalcoholic households: Relation to adolescent health symptomatology and problematic drinking. *Family Relations, 42,* 187–192.

Fiese, B. H. (2000). Family matters: A systems view of family effects on children's cognitive health. In R. J. Sternberg and E. L. Grigorenko (Eds.), *Environmental effects on cognitive abilities* (pp. 39–57). Mahwah, N.J.: Lawrence Erlbaum.

Fiese, B. H. (2002). Routines of daily living and rituals in family life: A glimpse at stability and change during the early school years. *Zero to Three, 22,* 10–13.

Fiese, B. H., Hooker, K. A., Kotary, L., and Schwagler, J. (1993). Family rituals in the early stages of parenthood. *Journal of Marriage and the Family, 57,* 633–642.

Fiese, B. H., and Kline, C. A. (1993). Development of the Family Ritual Questionnaire: Initial reliability and validation studies. *Journal of Family Psychology, 6,* 1–10.

Fiese, B. H., and Marjinsky, K. A. T. (1999). Dinnertime stories: Connecting relationship beliefs and child behavior. In B. H. Fiese, A. J. Sameroff, H. D. Grotevant, F. S. Wamboldt, S. Dickstein, and D. Fravel (Eds.), *The stories that families tell: Narrative coherence, narrative interaction, and relationship beliefs.* Monographs of the Society for Research in Child Development (Vol. 64 [2], Serial no. 257, pp. 52–68). Malden, Mass.: Blackwell.

Fiese, B. H., and Tomcho, T. (2001). Finding meaning in religious holiday rituals: Relation to marital satisfaction. *Journal of Family Psychology, 15,* 597–609.

Fiese, B. H., and Wamboldt, F. S. (2001). Family routines, rituals, and asthma management: A proposal for family based strategies to increase treatment adherence. *Families, Systems, and Health, 18,* 405–418.

Fiese, B. H., and Wamboldt, F. S. (2003). Tales of pediatric asthma management: Family based strategies related to medical adherence and health care utilization. *Journal of Pediatrics, 143,* 457–462.

Fiese, B. H., Wamboldt, F. S., and Anbar, R. D. (2005). Family Asthma Management Routines: Connections to medical adherence and quality of life. *Journal of Pediatrics, 146,* 171–176.

Fisher, L., and Weihs, K. L. (2000). Can addressing family relationships improve outcomes in chronic disease? *Journal of Family Practice, 49,* 561–566.

Fivush, R., Haden, C., and Reese, E. (1996). Remembering, recounting, and reminiscing: The development of autobiographical memory in social context. In D. C. Rubin (Ed.), *Remembering our past: Studies in autobiographical memory* (pp. 341–359). New York: Cambridge University Press.

Focht-Birkerts, L., and Beardslee, W. R. (2000). A child's experience of parental depression: Encouraging relational resilience in families with an affective illness. *Family Process, 39,* 417–434.

Fonagy, P. (2000). Attachment and borderline personality disorder. *Journal of the American Psychoanalytic Association, 48,* 1129–1146.

Frare, M., Axia, G., and Battistella, P. A. (2002). Quality of life, coping strategies, and family routines in children with chronic headache. *Headache, 42,* 953–962.

Fuligini, A. J., Yip, T., and Tseng, V. (2002). The impact of family obligation on the daily activities and psychological well-being of Chinese American adolescents. *Child Development, 73,* 302–314.

Furstenberg, F. F., Cook, T. D., Eccles, J., Elder, G. H., and Sameroff, A. J. (1999). *Managing to make it: Urban families and adolescent success.* Chicago: University of Chicago Press.

Ge, X., Best, K. M., Conger, R. D., and Simons, R. L. (1996). Parenting behaviors and the occurrence and co-occurrence of adolescent depressive symptoms and conduct problems. *Developmental Psychology, 32,* 717–731.

Gerstle, J. F., Varenne, H., and Contento, I. (2001). Post-diagnosis family adaptation influences glycemic control in women with type 2 diabetes mellitus. *Journal of the American Dietetic Association, 101,* 918–922.

Gillis, J. R. (1996). Making time for family: The invention of family time(s) and the reinvention of family history. *Journal of Family History, 21,* 4–21.

Gleason, J. B., Perlmann, R. Y., and Greif, E. B. (1984). What's the magic word: Learning language through politeness routines. *Discourse Processes, 7,* 493–502.

Goodnow, J. (1997). Parenting and the transmission and internalization of values: From social-cultural perspectives to within-family analyses. In J. E. Grusec and L. Kuczynski (Eds.), *Parenting and children's internalization of values.* (pp. 333–361). New York: John Wiley.

Goodnow, J. (2002). Adding culture to studies of development: Toward changes in procedure and theory. *Human Development, 45,* 237–245.

Gorman-Smith, D., Tolan, P. H., Henry, D. B., and Florsheim, P. (2000). Patterns of family functioning and adolescent outcomes among urban African American and Mexican American families. *Journal of Family Psychology, 14,* 436–457.

Greene, S. M., Anderson, E. R., Hetherington, E. M., Forgatch, M. S., and DeGarmo, D. S. (2003). Risk and reslience after divorce. In F. Walsh (Ed.), *Normal Family Processes: Growing diversity and complexity* (3rd ed., pp. 96–120). New York: Guilford.

Grusec, J. E., Goodnow, J. J., and Cohen, L. (1996). Household work and the development of concern for others. *Developmental Psychology, 32,* 999–1007.

Guidubaldi, J., Cleminshaw, H. K., Perry, J. D., Nastasi, B. K., and Lightel, J. (1986). The role of selected family environment factors in children's post-divorce adjustment. *Family Relations, 35,* 141–151.

Guidubaldi, J., Perry, J. D., and Nastasi, B. K. (1987). Growing up in a divorced family: Initial and long-term perspectives on children's adjustment. In S. Oskamp (Ed.), *Family processes and problems: Social psychological aspects* (pp. 202–237). Newbury Park: Sage.

Hareven, T. (1985). Historical changes in the family and the life course: Implications for child development. In A. B. Smuts and J. W. Hagen (Eds.), *History and research in child development.* Monographs of the Society for Research in Child Development (Vol. 50, pp. 8–23). Chicago: University of Chicago Press.

Harwood, R. L., Miller, A. M., Carlson, V. J., and Leyendecker, B. (2002). Child-rearing beliefs and practices during feed among middle-class Puerto Rican and Anglo mother-infant pairs. In J. M. Contreras, K. A. Kerns, and A. Neal-Barnett (Eds.), *Latino children and families in the United States: Current research and future directions* (pp. 133–153). Westport, Conn.: Praeger.

Hellbrugge, T., Lange, J. E., Rutenfranz, J., and Stehr, K. (1964). Circadian periodicity of physiological functions in different stages of infancy and childhood. *Annals of the New York Academy of Science, 117,* 361–373.

Henry, C. S., and Lovelace, S. G. (1995). Family resources and adolescent family life satisfaction in remarried family households. *Journal of Family Issues, 16,* 765–786.

Hetherington, E. M., and Kelly, J. (2002). *For better or for worse: Divorce reconsidered.* New York: Norton.

Hockenberger, E. H., Goldstein, H., and Hass, L. S. (1999). Effects of commenting during joint book reading by mothers with low SES. *Topics in Early Childhood Special Education, 19,* 15–27.

Hofferth, S. L., and Sandberg, J. F. (2001). How American children spend their time. *Journal of Marriage and Family, 63,* 295–308.

Howe, G. W. (2002). Integrating family routines and rituals with other family research paradigms: Comment on special section. *Journal of Family Psychology, 16,* 437–440.

Huston, A. C., Wright, J. C., Marquis, J., and Green, S. B. (1999). How young children spend their time: Television and other activities. *Developmental Psychology, 35,* 912–925.

Imber-Black, E. (2003). Ritual themes in families and family therapy. In E. Imber-Black, J. Roberts, and R. A. Whiting (Eds.), *Rituals in families and family therapy.* (2nd ed., pp. 49–87). New York: Norton.

Imber-Black, E., Roberts, J., and Whiting, R. A. (Eds.). (2003). *Rituals in families and family therapy.* (2nd ed.). New York: Norton.

Johnson, S. L., and Birch, L. L. (1994). Parents' and children's adiposity and eating style. *Pediatrics, 94,* 653–661.

Kalmijn, M. (2004). Marriage rituals as reinforcers of role transitions: An analysis of weddings in the Netherlands. *Journal of Marriage and Family, 66,* 582–594.

Kazdin, A. (Ed.). (2003). *Evidence-based psychotherapies for children and adolescents.* New York: Guilford.

Keltner, B. (1990). Family characteristics of preschool social competence among black children in a Head Start program. *Child Psychiatry and Human Development, 21,* 95–108.

Keltner, B. R. (1992). Family influences on child health status. *Pediatric Nursing, 18,* 128–131.

Kiecolt-Glaser, J. K., McGuire, L., Robler, T., and Glaser, R. (2002). Psychoneuroimmunology: Psychological influences on immune function and health. *Journal of Consulting and Clinical Psychology, 70,* 537–547.

Kim, S. Y., and Ge, X. (2000). Parenting practices and adolescent depressive symptoms in Chinese American families. *Journal of Family Psychology, 14,* 420–435.

Kirchler, E., Rodler, C., Holzl, E., and Meier, K. (2001). *Conflict and decision-making in close relationships: Love, money and daily routines.* East Sussex, England: Psychology Press.

Klass, C. S. (2003). *The home visitor's guidebook.* (2nd ed.). Baltimore: Paul H. Brookes.

Kroska, A. (2003). Investigating gender differences in the meaning of household chores and child care. *Journal of Marriage and Family, 65,* 456–473.

Kubicek, L. F. (2002). Fresh perspectives on young children and family routines. *Zero to Three, 22,* 4–9.

Kuhn, B. R., and Weidinger, D. (2000). Interventions for infant and toddler sleep disturbance: A review. *Child and Family Behavior Therapy, 22,* 33–50.

Larson, R., Dworkin, J., and Gillman, S. (2001). Facilitating adolescents' constructive use of time in one-parent families. *Applied Developmental Science, 5,* 143–157.

Leach, M. S., and Braithwaite, D. O. (1996). A binding tie: Supportive communication of family kinkeepers. *Journal of Applied Communication Research, 24,* 200–216.

Lee, E. J., Murry, V. M., Brody, G., and Parker, V. (2002). Maternal resources, parenting, and dietary patterns among rural African American children in single-parent families. *Public Health Nursing, 19,* 104–111.

Leon, K., and Jacobvitz, D. B. (2003). Relationships between adult attachment representations and family ritual quality: A prospective, longitudinal study. *Family Process, 42,* 419–432.

Lieberman, S. A. (1991). *New Traditions.* New York: Farrar, Straus and Giroux.

Lubeck, R. C., and Chandler, L. K. (1990). Organizing the home caregiving environment for infants. *Education and the Treatment of Children, 13,* 347–363.

Lucyshyn, J. M., Kayser, A. T., Irvin, L. K., and Blumberg, E. R. (2002). Functional assessment and positive behavior support at home with families: Defining effective and contextually appropriate behavior support plans. In J. M. Lucyshyn and G. Dunlap (Eds.), *Families and positive behavior support: Addressing problem behavior in family contexts.* (pp. 97–132). Baltimore: Paul H. Brookes.

Ludwig, F. M. (1998). The unpackaging of routine in older women. *American Journal of Occupational Therapy, 52,* 168–175.

Main, M., and Goldwyn, R. (1996). An adult classification system. Unpublished manual. University of California, Berkeley.

Markus, H. R., and Kitayama, S. (1994). A collective fear of the collective: Implications for selves and theories of selves. *Personality and Social Psychology Bulletin, 20,* 568–579.

Martinez, C. R., and Forgatch, M. S. (2001). Preventing problems with boys' noncompliance: Effects of a parent training intervention for divorcing mothers. *Journal of Consulting and Clinical Psychology, 69,* 416–428.

Martini, M. (1996). "What's New?" at the dinner table: Family dynamics during mealtimes in two cultural groups in Hawaii. *Early Development and Parenting, 5,* 23–34.

Martini, M. (2002). How mothers in four American cultural groups shape infant learning during mealtimes. *Zero to Three, 22,* 14–20.

McGoldrick, M., and Carter, B. (2003). The family life cycle. In F. Walsh (Ed.), *Normal Family Processes.* (3rd ed., pp. 375–398). New York: Guilford.

Mead, M. (1928). *Coming of age in Samoa.* Oxford: Morrow.

Meske, C., Sanders, G. F., Meredith, W. H., and Abbott, D. A. (1994). Perceptions of rituals and traditions among elderly persons. *Activities, Adaptation, and Aging, 18,* 13–26.

Milan, M. A., Mitchell, Z. P., Berger, M. I., and Pierson, D. F. (1981). Positive routines: A rapid alternative to extinction for elimination of bedtime tantrum behavior. *Child Behavior Therapy, 3,* 13–25.

Miller, P. J., Fung, H., and Mintz, J. (1996). Self-construction through narrative practices: A Chinese and American comparison of early socialization. *Ethos, 24,* 237–280.

Miller, P. J., Sandel, T. L., Liang, C., and Fung, H. (2001). Narrating transgressions in Longwood: The discourses, meanings, and paradoxes of an American socializing practice. *Ethos, 29,* 159–186.

Miller, P. J., Wiley, A. R., Fung, H., and Liang, C. (1997). Personal storytelling as a medium of socialization in Chinese and American families. *Child Development, 68,* 557–568.

Mindell, J. A. (1993). Sleep disorders in children. *Health Psychology, 12,* 151–162.

Minuchin, S. (1974). *Families and family therapy.* Cambridge, Mass.: Harvard University Press.

Napolitano, V. (1997). Becoming a Mujercita: Rituals, fiestas, and religious discourses. *Journal of the Royal Anthropological Institute, 3,* 279–296.

NIH. (1997). Guidelines for the diagnosis and management of asthma (NIH Publication No. 97-4051). Washington, D.C.: National Institutes of Health.

Nucci, L., and Smetana, J. G. (1996). Mothers' concepts of young children's areas of personal freedom. *Child Development, 67,* 1870–1886.

Olds, D. L. (2002). Prenatal and infancy home visiting by nurses: From randomized trials to community replication. *Prevention Science, 3,* 153–172.

Oliveri, M., and Reiss, D. (1987). Social networks of family members: Distinctive roles of mothers and fathers. *Sex Roles, 17,* 719–736.

Oswald, R. F. (2000). A member of the wedding? Heterosexism and family ritual. *Journal of Social and Personal Relationships, 17,* 349–368.

Oswald, R. F. (2002a). Inclusion and belonging in the family rituals of gay and lesbian people. *Journal of Family Psychology, 16,* 428–436.

Oswald, R. F. (2002b). Who am I in relation to them? Gay, lesbian, and queer people leave the city to attend rural family weddings. *Journal of Family Issues, 23,* 323–348.

Pachter, L. M., Cloutier, M. M., and Bernstein, B. A. (1996). Ethnomedical (folk) remedies for childhood asthma in a mainland Puerto Rican community. *Archives of Pediatrics and Adolescent Medicine, 149,* 982–988.

Parke, R. D. (2000). Beyond white and middle class: Cultural variations in families-assessments, processes, and policies. *Journal of Family Psychology, 14,* 331–333.

Parke, R. D., and O'Neil, R. (1999). Social relationships across contexts. In W. A. Collins and B. Laursen (Eds.), *Relationships as developmental contexts.* The Minnesota symposia on child psychology (Vol 30, pp. 211–239). Mahwah, N.J.: Lawrence Erlbaum.

Patterson, G. R. (1982). *Coercive family process.* Eugene, Ore.: Castalia.

Patterson, G. R., DeGarmo, D. S., and Forgatch, M. S. (2004). Systematic changes in families following prevention trials. *Journal of Abnormal Child Psychology, 32,* 621–633.

Patterson, J., and Garwick, A. (1994). Levels of meaning in family stress theory. *Family Process, 33,* 287–304.

Peterson, J. L., and Peterson, M. (2003). *The sleep fairy.* Omaha, Neb.: Behave'n Kids.

Pett, M. A., Lang, N., and Gander, A. (1992). Late-life divorce: Its impact on family rituals. *Journal of Family Issues, 13,* 526–552.

Pleck, E. (2000). *Celebrating the Family: Ethnicity, Consumer Culture and Family Ritual.* Cambridge, Mass.: Harvard University Press.

Popenoe, D. (1993). American family decline, 1960–1990: A review and appraisal. *Journal of Marriage and the Family, 55,* 527–542.

Porter, C. L., and Hsu, H. (2003). First-time mothers' perceptions of efficacy during the transition to motherhood: Links to infant temperament. *Journal of Family Psychology, 17,* 54–64.

Portes, P. R., Howell, S. C., Brown, J. H., Eichenberger, S., and Mas, C. A. (1992). Family functions and children's postdivorce adjustment. *American Journal of Orthopsychiatry, 62,* 613–617.

Presser, H. B. (1994). Employment schedules among dual-earner spouses and the division of household labor by gender. *American Sociological Review, 59,* 348–364.

Putnam, R. D. (2000). *Bowling alone: The collapse and revival of American community.* New York: Simon and Schuster.

Quittner, A. L., DiGirolamo, A. M., Michel, M., and Eigen, H. (1992). Parental response to cystic fibrosis: A contextual analysis of the diagnosis phase. *Journal of Pediatric Psychology, 17,* 683–704.

Quittner, A. L., Espelage, D. L., Opipari, L. C., Carter, B., Eid, N., and Eigen, H. (1998). Role strain in couples with and without a child with a chronic illness: Associations with marital satisfaction, intimacy, and daily mood. *Health Psychology, 17,* 112–124.

Ramey, S. L., and Juliusson, H. K. (1998). Family dynamics at dinner: A natural context for revealing basic family processes. In M. Lewis and C. Feiring (Eds.), *Families, risk, and competence.* (pp. 31–52). Mahwah, N.J.: Lawrence Erlbaum.

Reiss, D. (1981). *The family's construction of reality.* Cambridge, Mass.: Harvard University Press.

Reiss, D. (1989). The practicing and representing family. In A. J. Sameroff and R. Emde (Eds.), *Relationship disturbances in early childhood.* (pp. 191–220). New York: Basic Books.

Resnick, M. D., Bearman, P. S., Blum, R. W., Bauman, K. E., Harris, K. M., Jones, J., et al. (1997). Protecting adolescents from harm: Findings from the National Longitudinal Study of Adolescent Health. *JAMA, 278,* 823–832.

Richlin-Klonsky, J., and Bengston, V. L. (1996). Pulling together, drifting apart: A longitudinal case study of a four-generation family. *Journal of Aging Studies, 10,* 255–279.

Rideout, V. J., Vandewater, E. A., and Wartella, E. A. (2003). *Zero to Six: Electronic media in the lives of infants, toddlers, and preschoolers.* (No. 3378). Washington, D.C.: Kaiser Family Foundation.

Roberts, J. (2003). Setting the frame: Definition, functions, and typology of rituals. In E. Imber-Black, J. Roberts, and R. Whiting (Eds.), *Rituals in families and family therapy.* (Rev. ed., pp. 3–48). New York: Norton.

Roosa, M. W., Morgan-Lopez, A. A., Cree, W. K., and Specter, M. M. (2002). Ethnic culture, poverty, and context: Sources of influence on Latino families and children. In J. Contreras, K. Kerns, and A. Neal-Barnett (Eds.), *Latino children and families in the United States: Current research and future directions* (pp. 27–44). Westport, Conn.: Praeger.

Rosenthal, C. J., and Marshall, V. W. (1988). Generational transmission of family ritual. *American Behavioral Scientist, 31,* 669–684.

Roy, K. M., Tubbs, C. Y., and Burton, L. M. (2004). Don't have no time: Daily rhythms and the organization of time for low-income families. *Family Relations, 53,* 168–178.

Rutter, M., and Sroufe, L. A. (2000). Developmental psychopathology: Concepts and challenges. *Development and Psychopathology, 12,* 265–296.

Sameroff, A. J. (1987). The social context of development. In N. Eisenberg (Ed.), *Contemporary topics in developmental psychology.* (pp. 273–291). New York: Wiley.

Sameroff, A. J. (1995). General systems theories and developmental psychopathology. In D. Cicchetti and D. Cohen (Eds.), *Handbook of developmental psychopathology* (Vol. 1, pp. 659–695). New York: Wiley.

Sameroff, A. J., and Chandler, M. J. (1975). Reproductive risk and the continuum of caretaking causality. In F. D. Horowitz, M. Hetherington, S. Scarr-Salapetek, and G. Siegel (Eds.), *Review of child development research* (Vol. 4, pp. 187–244). Chicago: University of Chicago Press.

Sameroff, A. J., and Fiese, B. H. (1992). Family representations of development. In I. Sigel, McGillicuddy-DeLisi, and J. J. Goodnow (Eds.), *Parent belief systems: The psychological consequences for children.* (pp. 347–369). Hillsdale, N.J.: Lawrence Erlbaum.

Sameroff, A. J., and Fiese, B. H. (2000). Transactional regulation: The developmental ecology of early intervention. In S. J. Meisels and J. P. Shonkoff (Eds.), *Early intervention: A handbook of theory, practice, and analysis.* (pp. 3–19). New York: Cambridge University Press.

Sanders, M. R., Turner, K. M. T., Wall, C. R., Waugh, L. M., and Tully, L. A. (1997). Mealtime behavior and parent-child interaction: A comparison of children with cystic fibrosis, children with feeding problems, and non-clinic controls. *Journal of Pediatric Psychology, 22,* 881–900.

Seaton, E. K., and Taylor, R. D. (2003). Exploring familial processes in urban, low-income African American families. *Journal of Family Issues, 24,* 627–644.

Selvini-Palazzoli, M. S., Boscolo, L., Cecchin, G., and Pratta, G. (1977). Family rituals as a powerful tool in family therapy. *Family Process, 16,* 445–453.

Serpell, R., Sonnenschein, S., Baker, L., and Ganapathy, H. (2002). Intimate culture of families in the early socialization of literacy. *Journal of Family Psychology, 16,* 391–405.

Snawerdt, S. (2002). National poll shows family gatherings important to most Americans. Retrieved September 23, 2004, from www.gatherings.info/pressroom/release3.asp.

Snow, C. E., Dickinson, D. K., and Tabors, P. D. (1991). Early literacy: Linkages between home, school, and literacy achievement. *Journal of Research in Childhood Education, 6,* 1–46.

Speith, L. E., Stark, L. J., Mitchell, M. J., Schiller, M., Cohen, L. L., Mulvihill, M., and Hovell, M. F. (2001). Observational assessment of family functioning at mealtime in preschool children with cystic fibrosis. *Journal of Family Psychology, 26,* 215–224.

Sprunger, L. W., Boyce, W. T., and Gaines, J. A. (1985). Family-infant congruence: Routines and rhythmicity in family adaptations to a young infant. *Child Development, 56,* 564–572.

Steinglass, P. (1998). Multiple family discussion groups for patients with chronic medical illness. *Families, Systems, and Health, 16,* 55–70.

Steinglass, P., Bennett, L. A., Wolin, S. J., and Reiss, D. (1987). *The alcoholic family.* New York: Basic Books.

Sudarkasa, N. (1988). Interpreting the African heritage in Afro-American family organization. In H. P. McAdoo (Ed.), *Black families* (pp. 27–42). Newbury Park, Calif.: Sage.

Sytsma, S. E., Kelley, M. L., and Wymer, J. H. (2001). Development and initial validation of the child routines inventory. *Journal of Psychopathology and Behavioral Assessment, 23,* 241–251.

Taylor, R. D. (1996). Adolescents' perceptions of kinship support and family management practices: Association with adolescent adjustment in African American families. *Developmental Psychology, 32,* 687–695.

Taylor, R. D., and Roberts, D. (1995). Kinship support and maternal and adolescent well-being in economically disadvantaged African American families. *Child Development, 66,* 1585–1597.

Taylor, R. L. (2000). Diversity within African American families. In D. H. Demo, K. R. Allen, and M. A. Fine (Eds.), *Handbook of family diversity* (pp. 232–251). New York: Oxford University Press.

Teachman, J. D., Tedrow, L. M., and Crowder, K. D. (2000). The changing demography of America's families. *Journal of Marriage and the Family, 62,* 1234–1246.

Treudley, M. B. (1946). Mental illness and family routines. *Mental Hygiene, 30,* 235–249.

Turner, V. (1969). *The ritual process.* Chicago: Aldine.

Uttal, L. (1999). Using kin for child care: Embedment in the socioeconomic networks of extended families. *Journal of Marriage and the Family, 61,* 845–857.

van der Hart, O. (1983). *Rituals in psychotherapy: Transitions and continuity.* New York: Irvington.

van der Hart, O., Witztum, E., and de Voogt, A. (1988). Myths and rituals: Anthropological views and their application in strategic family therapy. *Journal of Psychotherapy and the Family, 4,* 57–79.

Visher, E. B., Visher, J. S., and Palsey, J. (2003). Remarriage families and stepparenting. In F. Walsh (Ed.), *Normal family processes: Growing diversity and complexity* (3rd ed., pp. 153–175). New York: Guilford.

Vuchinich, S. (1987). Starting and stopping spontaneous family conflicts. *Journal of Marriage and the Family, 49,* 591–601.

Vuchinich, S., Emery, R. E., and Cassidy, J. (1988). Family members as third parties in dyadic family conflict: Strategies, alliances, and outcomes. *Child Development, 59,* 1293–1302.

Walter, M. P. (1995). *Kwanzaa: A family affair.* New York: Lothrop, Lee and Shepard.

Wamboldt, F. S., and Reiss, D. (1989). Defining a family heritage and a new relationship identity: Two central tasks in the making of a marriage. *Family Process, 28,* 317–335.

Wamboldt, F. S., Wamboldt, M. Z., Gavin, L. A., Roesler, L. A., and Brugman, S. M. (1995). Parental criticism and treatment outcome in adolescents hospitalized for severe, chronic asthma. *Journal of Psychosomatic Research, 39,* 995–1005.

Weisner, T. S. (2002). Ecocultural understanding of children's developmental pathways. *Human Development, 45,* 275–281.

Whiteside, M. F. (2003). Creation of family identity through ritual performances in early remarriage. In E. Imber-Black, J. Roberts and R. A. Whiting (Eds.), *Rituals in families and family therapy* (pp. 300–329). New York: Norton.

Wolcott, J. Reports of demise of family dinner are greatly exaggerated; some 63% of American families eat dinner together often or always. *Christian Scientist Monitor,* September 5, 2001, p. 15.

Wolin, S. J., and Bennett, L. A. (1984). Family rituals. *Family Process, 23,* 401–420.

Wolin, S. J., Bennett, L. A., and Jacobs, J. S. (2003). Assessing family rituals in alcoholic families. In E. Imber-Black, J. Roberts,, and R. A. Whiting (Eds.), *Rituals in families and family therapy* (Rev. ed., pp. 253–279). New York: Norton.

Wolin, S. J., Bennett, L. A., Noonan, D. L., and Teitlebaum, M. A. (1980). Disrupted family rituals: A factor in generational transmission of alcoholism. *Journal of Studies of Alcohol, 41,* 199–214.

Yoos, H. L., Kitzman, H., and Cole, R. (1999). Family routines and the feeding process. In D. B. Kessler and P. Dawson (Eds.), *Failure to thrive and pediatric undernutrition: A transdisciplinary approach.* (pp. 375–384). Baltimore: Paul H. Brookes.

Index

abuse, 117, 121

academic achievement, 56, 98, 103, 128

achievement expectations, 67

adolescents, 38, 61, 86; conflict in girls, 58–59; feelings of alienation, 59, 73, 98, 134; health and well-being, 77, 84; importance of routines and rituals, 57–59; mental health issues, 57–58; obligations to family, 73; parental alcohol use and, 97; parental depression and, 105; problem solving with, 35; remarriage and, 98; risky behavior, 128; security and identity issues, 61; time negotiations by, 62

adoption, 109

Adult Attachment Interview, 48

affect: of children, 4, 50, 85; investment in, 127; meals and, 19, 24, 52, 101; in routines and rituals, 90, 107, 108, 122, 123, 125, 129, 131; affirming activities, 59

African-American families: behavior problems, 56; extended-kin networks, 73–75; in poverty, 56, 103; routines in family life, 56

aggression, 108

alcohol use, 57, 84, 93, 105; effect on family rituals, 95–97; transmission of, 94, 96

alienation, 59, 73, 98, 134

ambiguity, 40, 60

anorexia nervosa, 108

attachment theory, 7, 48–49

authority, 17

baptisms, 25

Bar Mitzvah, 69, 71

Bat Mitzvah, 69

bedtime routines, 5, 26, 27, 32, 51, 56; chronic illness and, 84–85; disruption of, 113–114, 124; divorce and, 98; family therapy and, 113–114, 115;

positive, 113; poverty and, 104; reading stories, 40, 114, 119, 136

behavior, 4, 6, 64, 78; changes, 3, 86, 104, 107, 115, 117, 118, 122, 124; codes of, 126; cultural mores and, 13; directly observed, 8, 10, 13, 17, 18, 27; influenced by family beliefs, 8–9; monitoring of, 127, 128–129; personal transgressions, 64, 67–68, 76; predictions of, 131; problems, 7, 53, 107, 112, 128–129; regulation, 5, 119; social influences on, 6–7; tantrums, 113, 124

biology, 126, 127–128

birthdays, 98

births, 4, 5; disruption of routines and rituals by, 49–50; premature, 6, 105–106

bisexual family members, 45

Blum-Kulka, Shoshana, 65–66

Boll, Eleanor Stoker, 32–36, 99, 136

Bossard, James H. S., 32–36, 99, 136

breastfeeding, 6, 50–51

caregivers, 6, 33, 89; burdens on, 53, 90, 91; grandmothers as, 59, 74, 102; high-risk children and, 93, 95; for infants and toddlers, 7–8, 61; routines for, 50, 51, 52

celebrations: *see* holidays and celebrations

change in families, 2, 4, 9, 27, 62, 134; adaptive, 96–97; challenges of, 5, 118; cultural, 71; economic, 3, 71; family organization, 34–36; flexibility in, 96–97; reassignment of roles, 76; structural shifts, 29; unanticipated, 5. *See also* behavior: changes

child care, 103, 105, 135; extended-kin networks and, 74; facilities, 105; poverty and, 101–104; routines, 50; women as providers of, 33

child development, 2, 3, 5, 27, 79; cultural expectations for, 15; language

DISCARD

DATE DUE
